321914

D0518511

181 E

Learning and
Teaching Swimming

Joseph McKeown

Learning and teaching swimming

Illustrated by Andrew McKeown

Adlard Coles Limited   London

Granada Publishing Limited
First published in Great Britain 1973
by Adlard Coles Limited
Frogmore, St Albans, Hertfordshire AL2 2NF and
3 Upper James Street, London W1R 4BP

ISBN 0 229 11522 5

Made and printed in Great Britain by Tinling (1973) Ltd.,
Prescot, Lancs. (a member of the Oxley Printing Group).

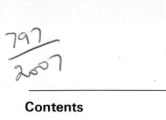

Contents

Illustrations

Acknowledgements

My wife Margorie
My sons Andrew and Duncan
Mr B Allinson and the staff of the Cambridge Parkside Pool
Mr N C Nicholes of the Cambridge Grammar School for Boys
Alderman H E Fern, CBE, JP, Hon. Life president ASA, founder
member FINA
Mr F Quinney, Chairman of Cambridge and Ely RNLSS
Mr D Figg, Senior National Technical Officer RNLSS
The many pupils who have worked so hard
To you all, many thanks for your valuable cooperation in the
preparation of this book

1

Essentials of teaching

The teacher's first duty, whether he is instructing a single pupil or a class, is to ensure safety. A single pupil will cause little problem, but with a class of excited children you must give more attention to this. Without cracking the whip too hard, ensure that you always have *discipline.* You must have instant obedience to your signals and a sharp word for anyone who starts pushing another pupil in the water. There is usually *one* pupil who will upset the whole class if he is not checked immediately. In case someone is hurt in spite of all your efforts, make sure that you are familiar with the swimming bath's emergency arrangements. Don't panic: bath attendants in my experience are both efficient and cooperative so you should go to them immediately for help. The best remedy is still prevention so always have firm control of your class.

Whether you are taking a class or an individual, your pupils *must* enjoy the lesson if it is to be successful. If they don't, they will never learn how to swim and they will also become bored. Always prepare your lesson beforehand. If it is not prepared your pupils will not be fooled, as children spot a phoney quicker than anyone. Give your lesson a little thought to make it varied and enjoyable. Be firm but gentle, and laugh with them, not at them.

The water is a fearful new element to timid children so don't try to bully them into swimming as it won't work. You may even put them off for life. Sticking rigidly to an idea or set of practices becomes boring for teacher and pupil, so make the lesson flexible, experiment, adapt and be resourceful. Finally, the lesson practices contained in the individual sections of this book are only guides. Use them and adapt them to suit your purposes, but do *not* stick slavishly to them. Every child has different abilities, mental approach and physical make-up. This book contains something for all of them, but you as the teacher should select what is suitable for your pupil and to put it over to him.

Always arrange demonstrations where possible for parts of a

stroke and then for the whole movement. After this allow the pupil to attempt the whole skill so that you can assess the practices most beneficial to him. Take your pupil through the practices as described in the various sections.

Giving the pupil confidence

The complete beginner's main problem is one of confidence. There are as many ways of imparting this as there are pupils and teachers, so it is purely an individual art. This problem is less acute when you are teaching a class, because you can effectively use the abilities of one pupil to stimulate the efforts of another. If you are dealing with a single pupil who is literally terrified of the water, you will need considerable acumen and patience just to get him immersed. Whatever the problems you face with a beginner, *never* rush it, don't cajole or force, and try to keep the proceedings on a fairly light-hearted level.

If the beginner is an adult, you will have an additional problem. As well as being frightened of the water he will be afraid of making himself look ridiculous. Once again, your approach must be an individual one and no particular rule can be laid down. However, a persuasive tongue, flexibility, patience and a ready supply of common-sense are always great assets.

By using the following well-tried methods you will usually succeed in getting any pupil into shallow water.

Practices for first entries

a   Sit on the side, dangling the feet in the water
b   Get the pupil to work his way down the steps backwards. Hold him if necessary
c   Sit on the side. Bend and hold the rail then slide in, still holding on to it
d   Sit on the side with your partner standing in the water. Hold the pupil either by the hand or round the waist and help him to slide in facing forwards
e   Lie on the stomach with the back to the water. The legs should be dangling and the hands gripping the surround. Slide in backwards keeping contact with the side with or without a partner, as in d.

Gaining confidence in the water

As soon as the pupil is in the water reduce his fear of it as quickly as possible. Get him moving about so he can feel the water swirling about him. The following exercises are helpful in achieving this aim:

a   Holding the rail or free-standing, crouch to shoulder level and then stand up

b   Holding the rail or free-standing, breathe in and then immerse the face up to the ears

c   Place the hands on the knees, breathe in and put the whole face in the water

d   Place the hands on the knees and breathe in. Bend at the waist, submerge and then stand up

e   Standing in the water, breathe in and bend to touch the toes. Submerge and then stand up

f   Stand in the water, breathe in and then submerge to go on the hands and knees on the bottom. Stand up again

g   If the water is shallow enough, put the hands on the bottom and let the legs float freely behind

h   Jump up and down occasionally crouching and submerging

Getting the feet off the bottom

Always take it gently when getting the pupil to take his feet off the bottom. If your pupil submerges with his mouth open while he is breathing in, it could set him back for weeks and all your earlier work will have been wasted. To prevent this happening during early experiments at taking his feet off the bottom load him with sufficient artificial aids such as rubber rings and arm bands, to render him unsinkable. One of the constant delights of teaching children is to see the change that comes over them when they suddenly realise that they *cannot* sink. Their faces light up and they thrash gleefully about. Before they realise it their feet are off the bottom and they are floating freely in the water.

Let your pupil enjoy himself in his new element for a while. This free movement in the water with the certainty that he cannot sink is worth a million words from the teacher. After a short period of freedom quietly call him to the side and remove the surplus aids. Ensure that you have left enough aids to maintain absolute safety from accidental ducking and then let him play again. Now observe him closely. Watch his natural limb movements and assess the stroke to which he would most readily adapt himself. Use suitable actions to demonstrate the leg and arm movements of different strokes and get him to imitate you. Watch for his natural reactions. Do *not* expect miracles at this stage, as his efforts will probably be feeble. Once he has taken the first step, it is up to you to encourage further progress. The rudimentary movements of all the teaching strokes can be dealt with in this play and you should assess your pupil's most natural movements during the exercises.

Regaining the feet

Once the pupil's reliance on artificial aids had been reduced to a minimum, teach him the simple but vital skill of regaining his feet from both prone (on the stomach) and the supine (on the back) positions. These two essential movements are often forgotten in early training, but they should not be left out. To regain the feet from the supine position keep the legs together and the arms sideways. Sweep the arms towards the feet, at the same time bending the knees to place the feet on the bottom. To regain the feet from the prone position, keep the legs together and sweep the arms from beyond the head directly under the body, at the same time bending the knees to place the feet on the bottom.

Work groups

The same basic procedure for introducing the pupil to swimming movements holds good for a whole class of beginners. Naturally teaching a class entails more work and observation for the teacher, but even at this stage it will begin to resolve itself into two or three groups according to ability, such as poor, fair and good.

Separate the pupils into these groups to begin actual stroke work. Do not make the groups into a permanent arrangement, as they *must* be flexible. For instance a pupil may be good at breaststroke and for this he would be in group A. He may be bad though at front crawl and for this he would be in group C. Few classes are of equal ability in all areas, at this stage or later on, so to attempt to keep your pupils in permanent groups for all stroke work would hold back some pupils on strokes to which they were not naturally adapted. Carefully selected ability groups make for greater success in class work, but they must be *carefully* selected.

At first it is easier and more effective to group your pupils according to their reactions to the water and particularly whether they are nervous or confident. In these groups you should assess the individual's most suitable starting stroke and, having selected it, split the class into ability groups. You will have three groups each for breaststroke, front crawl and back crawl work. The result is that the pupil who is naturally adapted to breaststroke, fair to poor in back crawl and hopeless at front crawl would be in the following work groups: breastroke group A, back crawl group B or C and front crawl group C. The groups would then change around according to which stroke you were teaching at a particular time.

Lesson preparation and timing

In stroke work there is always a certain degree of repetition, which is why I insisted that the lesson should be carefully prepared to prevent boredom. It is vital that the programme should have pace. The temperatures of the water and the surrounding air play a major part in teaching swimming. No child will work enthusiastically if he is cold and the colder the conditions, the shorter and more vigorous the lesson should be. In normal water with a temperature of approximately 78 degrees fahrenheit, lessons should last for twenty to thirty minutes. The whole of this time should be made as varied and enjoyable as possible. Remember finally that the class will mirror the teacher. If you are dull, so are they. If you are inefficient, then they will be inefficient too. In a good lesson time should fly and the class should leave the water anxious for their next lesson. If this does not happen, *examine yourself and your methods*, as something *must* be wrong somewhere.

Progress so far

a   The pupils know exactly where they stand regarding discipline
b   They are in the water and confident with aids
c   Their feet are off the bottom and they are moving freely
d   They can regain their feet from both prone and supine positions

The next step is to teach your pupils a simple prone supine and the mushroom float. These will add immeasurably to their confidence before they commence detailed stroke work and will materially reduce the time taken to learn to swim. Full details of all the floating techniques will be found in the chapter on floating. Now that we have completed an introduction to the basic skills, we can start teaching our beginners to swim effectively. Detailed teaching practices for each stroke have been described under individual stroke headings in the chapter on strokes.

2

Buoyancy in the water

Treading water

Your class should be taught how to tread water as early as possible because it is a basic skill in watermanship and can prove the saving factor between calm and fatal panic in an emergency. There should be no hurried movements or sudden jerks and the body should be submerged as much as possible. The object of all the body movements should be to press the water downwards.

The leg action can be either a simple opening and closing of the legs sideways, or a scissors kick putting one leg forwards and the other one backwards, and then bringing them together. In both of these movements the lower leg should give a circular swirl when closing with the other one. The arm action can consist of any movement provided that the hands are kept palm downwards and the movement presses the water downwards. These are the basic movements which should be adapted to suit the individual pupil.

Practices for beginners

a   Demonstrate the movements in the water
b   Get the pupil in shallow water up to chin level with inflatable arm-bands and doing leg movements to suit himself. He should be within reach of the teacher from the side of the pool
c   Repeat b, reducing the air in the aids. The hands can be anywhere between shoulder and waist level but must be palm-downwards
d   At the same depth, but within the teacher's reach, repeat this exercise without aids
e   Repeat d at a depth one foot above the pupil's height. First do it within reach of the side and then about three or four feet away from it. The teacher can hold a short stick in front of the pupil to give him extra confidence and then remove it when he feels more assured

f   Repeat exercise d in deep water, first with a stick and then without. Test the pupil's efficiency by timing him, building his ability to tread water up to three minutes
g   Vary the exercise by putting one arm behind the back and then both of them there, or placing the hands on the head or in the air
h   When g can be done efficiently add some clothing, such as a pyjama jacket, and then do it with the trousers as well. Build this up as the pupil's efficiency grows

Try to achieve quiet even movements with maximum limb support from the water. Aim at steady breathing and full use of the hands.

Floating

Floating is a basic essential of watermanship and should be taught as early as possible.

The mushroom or tucked float
a   Inhale deeply
b   Bend the trunk forward
c   Allow the head to hang in the water
d   Lift the feet gently and tuck them in to the bottom
e   Clasp the hands round the knees
f   Keep still in the position with minimum water disturbance
Do not jump into the tuck position.

Practices for beginners

a   Demonstrate the float in the water. Explain that there will be a slight rocking movement to and fro before the body eventually settles. The pupil must *not* open out when this happens but keep still in the tuck position
b   Standing in shallow water up to chest level. Breathe in deeply and bend forward from the waist. Put the head to the knees and submerge until running out of breath
c   Repeat a allowing the feet to drift off the bottom momentarily and then replacing them

d   Repeat b lifting the legs gently into the tuck and grasping the knees with the hands. Hold this for a full breath and then stand up

e   Repeat d two or three times gradually taking the water up to chin level

f   Push slowly from the side going first into a prone position and then to a tuck float position

g   Vary the exercise, for example as in f or by starting from a treading water position

Points to watch for with beginners

a   Breathing in well
b   Gentle movements
c   Allow the water to take the body's weight before lifting the feet as in exercise c above
d   Tight tuck position
e   Relaxation especially in the way the head hangs

Back floating (supine)

In the back float the legs tend to sink slowly, causing the hips to bend and the pupil to lose his balance. To offset this allow him to use a gentle hand scull and leg movement in the early stages, until he has gained confidence and mastered the technique.

Practices for beginners

a   Demonstration of the movement in the water
b   Get the pupil to try it out in shallow water with aids or with a partner's support. Place the toes under the rail, which should be grasped with both hands. Unroll gently to a horizontal position with the head comfortably resting on the water and the hands quietly sculling. When the body is balanced and relaxed release the toes. Repeat this several times gradually reducing the sculling
c   Repeat exercise b. When balance has been achieved push off gently from the side, sculling slightly if necessary until full confidence has been achieved

These exercises can also be practised with pole, rope or sling support. When the pupil is balanced horizontally the support should gradually be removed. If you have several pupils they should get into position and practise exercise b. Then get one of them to hold a light pole in the centre of the class under the learners' backs. When they are horizontally balanced the pole can be removed by pressing it downwards.

Points to watch for with learners

a   Relaxation
b   Flat body position
c   Head resting comfortably on the water
d   No bend in the hips
e   No bend in the knees
f   Hands close to the sides
g   Steady and even breathing
h   No arch in the back

Motionless float (supine)
Once the pupil can float on his back you can teach him the motionless float. This position is the same as for the back float, with the arms extended beyond the head.

Practices for beginners

a   Demonstrate the float
b   Run through the back float again until it is well balanced and motionless
c   Starting with the back float bring the arms to the sides and press gently down with the hands until the toes break the surface. The body should be horizontal
d   Repeat c and then gently move the arms out and round until they are extended beyond the head. All movements should then cease
e   Repeat until the pupil is proficient, testing this by timing the float

The same points should be watched for as with the back float, but you must also make sure that the extended arm movement is performed gently and evenly.

Spreadeagle float (supine)
The initial position for the spreadeagle float is the same as for

the motionless float. When the body is still, spread the arms and legs sideways and remain motionless holding the position. The same points should be watched for as in the motionless float, but also see that the spreading of the limbs is done gently and evenly.

Floating on the front (prone)
Floating on the front is good for conserving energy, although if the face is immersed it requires rather more control and confidence. The legs tend to sink slowly so learners can make gentle leg movements to maintain their balance. Watch out for the back arching due to leg movements, as it will upset the body balance completely if the arch becomes accentuated. When the legs sink it is usually better to let them go slowly, allowing the body to hang at an incline, as in this way the float will be held for a longer period.

If the pupil can do the mushroom float, use the following short cut to the prone and spreadeagle floats.
a   Tread water
b   Adopt the mushroom float position
c   Open the body and stretch
d   Spread the limbs sideways
All movements must be done gently.

If the pupil cannot perform a mushroom float the exercises which follow will help.

Practices for beginners

a   Stand with the water at chest level and holding the bar at arm's length. Breathe in, put the face in the water and then stand up
b   Hold the bar with one hand, keeping the other hand low down on the wall. Stretch the body in the prone float position then immerse the face in the water. Raise the head to breathe. Repeat this three or four times
c   The pupil should be in shallow water with aids or a partner's support if necessary. Starting from a prone float position, press the palms down gently to maintain balance and then raise the head to breathe. Repeat this exercise three or four times
d   Repeat c removing the support if possible

12

e   Get into the prone position and immerse the face, gently pushing off from the side to float

Points to watch for with learners

a   Complete relaxation
b   No arch in the back
c   A good breath should be taken before beginning the float
d   The palms should be flat in the water
e   Use the pressure of the palms to raise the head for breathing
f   No strain on the neck muscles
g   The body should be horizontal and balanced
h   All movement must be gentle, with minimum water disturbance

The spreadeagle float (prone)
Assume the prone float position and, when the body is still, spread the arms and legs gently sideways. The exercises are the same as for the prone float except that the limbs are spread.

The motionless float (prone)
To achieve the motionless float position, first do a prone float. When the body is motionless, move the arms from a sideways position until they are extended beyond the head to the width of the shoulders. This can be practised in the same way as the prone float, simply adding on the extended arm movement.

The vertical float
As it gives the maximum support to the body, the vertical float is an excellent one for survival purposes. The pupil hangs vertically in the water. His head should be tilted slightly backwards with only the nose and the mouth clear of the surface. This float requires good control and before teaching it you should be sure that the pupil can perform the other floats properly.

Practices for beginners

a   Demonstrate the float
b   Start at a depth where there is one clear foot of water beneath the standing pupil. He should be near the rail and

treading water. The teacher *must* control his movement into a vertical float

c   Repeat exercise b, gradually slowing down the movements. The teacher should control this until the pupil is motionless with his head tilted back and fully supported by the water

d   When he is confident the pupil can be taken into deep water to perform this float. A short stick held underwater within reach of the pupil builds up his confidence at this stage

Points to watch for with beginners

a   Complete relaxation
b   No strain in the neck muscles
c   Regular breathing
d   Maximum support should be gained from the water
e   No limb movement
f   No bend in the hips
g   No arch in the back

Once the pupil can float he should practise the floats in various positions, for example changing from the mushroom float to the prone float, or from the prone float rolling over into the supine float. There are many combinations of floating and treading water that can be practised and timed. Whatever variation is used, you must *insist* that all movements are carried out quietly and gently to maintain the good balance which is essential to successful floating. Further buoyancy exercises are described in the chapter on water games and tricks.

3
The Strokes

The breaststroke

Teach this stroke as a first stroke if you can to prevent possible
difficulty with the leg movement at a later stage. The arm and
leg movements occur simultaneously on the same level. The
body position should be almost horizontal with a slight incline
from the head to the feet. The legs are the main source of
propulsion and all movements are performed underwater.

Order of limb movement during the stroke

Start from the stretched position in the glide with the arms
beyond the head, the trunk and legs in line, the arms held
straight and the palms square to the line of the pull, then sweep
sideways and slightly downwards to a point just in front of the
shoulder line. The elbows bend and the hands are brought
across the chest to a point just in front of the chin. The arms
finally push forward into a glide position.
  As the arms are completing their pull to the shoulder line, the
knees bend, the heels are drawn up together to the bottom and
the toes cocked towards the knees. The legs kick out and round,
as the arms push forward to glide. The kick is completed with
full ankle extension as the legs come together, and the body is in
the glide position.

Demonstrations

Although progressive the practices suggested here are for guidance. How they should be used will depend upon the pupil's
ability. Demonstrations for this stroke are best viewed from
above and behind the swimmer, except for the arm movement
which can be seen from the front.
  To perform the leg movement from the glide position the
heels are drawn up to the bottom and the toes cocked towards
the knees, which are outside the body line. The legs kick out and

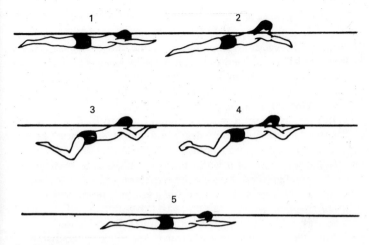

1 Breaststroke

round until they come together with a final extension of the ankle at the end of the kick.

Leg movement practices

a   Hold the rail and practise the leg movement. A partner can provide guidance if necessary. The teacher should check this movement

b   Hold the rail and repeat the movement slowly until it is correct, with the teacher checking the ankle play. When it is being done properly, start building up a rhythm

c   Practise the leg kick in the water with aids if required. The teacher should check and correct

d   Push off from the side. Put the face in the water and glide fully stretched to improve the balance

e   When exercise d can be done properly with aids, add three or four leg kicks, keeping the face clear of the water

f   Hold the rail as in a. Correct any faults in the kick before proceeding and if necessary do some ankle work on land to achieve greater flexibility. The aim of these exercises is to build a strong and correct kick with good balance

Arm stroke practices

Normally the swimmer breathes in at the end of the arm pull, which should be carried out with straight arms and a slightly downward pull to just in front of the shoulder line.

a   Standing in water up to chest level lean forward and practise the arm movement under the teacher's control
b   Repeat exercise a with individual control. The teacher should check for correct depth and line, straight arms and a shoulder line recovery point
c   Stand a quarter of a width from the side and then swim in. The teacher should check the stroke movements: the arms as the pupil approaches and the legs when he returns to his starting position
d   Return to the individual practices for fault correction
e   Push from the side into a full stroke building up the distance covered with increasing ability

The stroke rhythm should be steady and unhurried.

Points to watch for with new swimmers

Leg action
a   Toes cocked when the feet are drawn up
b   Knees outside the body line
c   Kick with the inner borders of the feet
d   Full use of the feet and ankles
e   Even and simultaneous movements on the same level
f   Kick starting slowly with the speed building up until it is vigorous at the end
g   Legs not too low in the water
h   Pause at the end of the kick

Arm action
a   Straight arm pull
b   Direction of pull should be slightly downwards and about twelve inches deep
c   Even pressure on the water and no snatching at it
d   Wrists firm throughout the pull
e   Extent of pull should be just in front of the shoulder line
f   Quick recovery from the end of the pull to the beginning of the glide push

Breathing
a   Whether breathing is naturally timed or too early or late
b   No holding of breath
c   Check the head position to see that it is not too far back
d   Breathe out as the arms push forward to glide

The front crawl

Although the front crawl is one of the most efficient strokes, it requires very good coordination because of the breathing. This means that careful work is needed during the initial stages of teaching the stroke, if you are to achieve the effortless movement which is its chief characteristic. Success in teaching this stroke depends not only on the quality of the teaching itself, but also on the physical make-up of the pupil, especially the strength and flexibility of his shoulder girdle. If the front crawl is taught as a first stroke, it may be difficult to teach the breaststroke at a later stage. Unless the pupil has a natural aptitude for front crawl, it is therefore advisable to commence the pupil's swimming tuition by teaching him the breaststroke.

The stroke consists of alternating arm movements and alternating leg movements in the vertical plane. The body position should be as flat and straight as possible in the prone position. The face should be in the water with a comfortable head position. The whole movement must be relaxed and unstrained.

Order of limb movement throughout the stroke

The legs and arms move independently. The arms work in a roughly circular direction from the point of entry and through the pulling stage under the body to the hip, where the arm is lifted out of the water and carried forward again to the point of entry. The pull must be made with the elbow bent and the arms are never straight in this stroke.

The legs perform a simple up and down movement to a depth of approximately eighteen inches below the surface. The movement starts in the hip and flows through the leg with a whip-like action, ending in a final flick through the flexible ankle joint. The interpretation of these basic movements will vary from one pupil

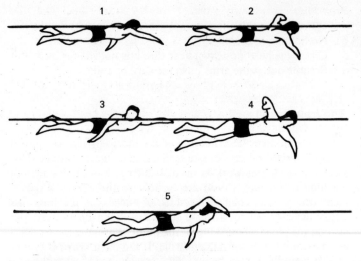

2   Front crawl

to another, depending on individual factors such as physical strength, shoulder mobility and breathing efficiency.

Demonstrations

Demonstrations for the front crawl stroke are best viewed as the swimmer passes the spectator. The leg actions can be seen from the side and rear, but the arm action is most visible from directly in front of the swimmer.

As an initial practice hold the float at arm's length beyond the head and practise the leg movement. Practise canoeing in a stretched position on the surface with the hands clasped behind the back and using only the legs. Finally do doggy paddle in the prone position, holding the head up and performing a crawl leg action with the arms alternately reaching forward and pulling under the body, which should be kept underwater throughout.

Leg movement practices

a   Hold the rail with the back of the hands to the wall and the elbows resting against it. Stretch the body just under the surface and slowly practise the leg kick. Check that the action is from the hip and that the knees are slightly flexed. Also make sure that there is good ankle play and that the toes have turned slightly inwards. There should be no arch in the back

b Repeat exercise a, holding the rail at arm's length with the face clear of the water
c Repeat b putting the face in and lifting the head clear of the water to breathe
d Push off from the side and glide with the face in to achieve good balance
e Push off from the side with a float and add the leg action. Do this for half a width and repeat it until the leg action is even and effective and the balance good
f Repeat c with the face in the water but turn the head to whichever side seems most natural to breathe
g Push off from the side and float with the face immersed. Perform the leg action and then turn the head to breathe
h Push off from the side into the canoe position. Roll sideways several times in a full circle using the legs only

Arm movement practices

a Push off from the side with aids if these seem to be necessary. Do the crawl leg stroke and the doggy paddle arm stroke, keeping the head up. Repeat this until it is correctly performed with no arch in the back
b Stand in shallow water with one leg forward. Lean forwards and practise the arm action. Check that the pupil has a comfortable reach with a slight bend in the elbow and that his fingers are going in first. The entry point should be between the shoulder and the centre line of the body with the arms pulling evenly under the body. The elbow should lift when the hand reaches the thigh and there should be a quick relaxed recovery to the re-entry point. The teacher should control this exercise
c Repeat b walking forwards with individual control
d Push off from the side adding the leg action and then two or three cycles of the arm action. The pupil's face should be in the water and he should not breathe in. Repeat this exercise increasing the strokes to the full extent of one breath

Breathing practices

Breathing should be demonstrated on land and in the water before commencing practices. The swimmer breathes as his hand passes his mouth on the pull.

a   With the rail at arm's length put the face in the water and turn the head to breathe either on the natural side or on alternate sides. Practise the leg movement only with a float and breathing as above
b   Push from the side and do the full stroke for a short distance. First breathe only once and repeat this
c   Repeat exercise b increasing the distance as the pupil's technique improves

Where possible the pupil should adopt the habit of breathing on alternate sides because it gives a flatter body position. Greater efficiency will be achieved if there is an even rhythm in his arm stroke. Any pupil able to breathe on only one side should practise pushing off with a float under his extended hand on the non-breathing side. He should perform the normal stroke with his free hand, breathing in during the correct part of it.

Front crawl breathing is the most difficult of the stroke techniques to master. Much will depend on the pupil's aptitude but his technique is absolutely vital. Some pupils prefer to breathe in and allow the air to trickle out into the water during the arm cycle, breathing in again on the next stroke. This is difficult for a beginner and may lengthen the time taken to master the stroke. The second and perhaps more natural method is called explosive breathing. The pupil breathes in, holds his breath until the arm cycle is completed, then forces it out and snatches a new one. Check which way of breathing is more instinctive to the pupil as the more natural the technique, the more efficient he will be.

Points to watch for with new swimmers

Leg action
a   Not too low
b   Good rhythm
c   Relaxation
d   Movement starting in the hip

e   The knees should not be bent too much
f   Feet kept under water
g   Approximately eighteen inches depth of kick
h   Ankle flexibility
i   Legs close together

Arm movement

a   Entry point of the hand
b   Slight bend in the elbow on entry
c   Fingers in first
d   Direction of pull should be straight under the body
e   High elbow lift for recovery
f   Elbow lift should be as the hand reaches the hip
g   No pause in the arm action
h   Even pressure on the pull with the hand square to the line of the pull
i   Relaxed shoulders used as a pivot

Breathing

a   The head turned rather than lifted to breathe
b   Timing of the actual breathing in the stroke cycle
c   Type of breathing most natural to the individual pupil

General

a   Flat body position
b   Comfortable head position with no strain in the neck muscles
c   Balanced position with no excessive rolling
d   Good rhythm
e   Complete relaxation

The back crawl

The breathing problems are considerably reduced in the back crawl. It is popular with learners and is often taught as a first stroke. Give close attention to your pupil during the confidence-building stage, as this may well be the stroke which will suit a particularly nervous beginner.

To perform the back crawl the body lies horizontally just beneath the surface. The head should rest comfortably on the surface with the ears covered and the face clear of the water. The shoulders should just break the surface while the knees remain submerged. The legs work in a simple up and down movement as in the front crawl, while the arms work alternately and continuously.

Order of limb movements during the stroke

The leg action is the same as for the front crawl, commencing in the hip and flowing whip-like through the leg. There should be a slight bend of the knees and a final flick through a flexible ankle joint. The toes are turned slightly inwards throughout the

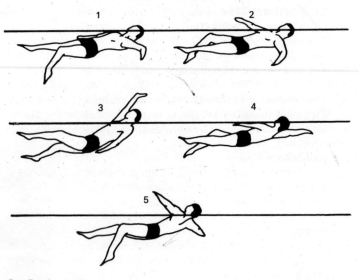

3 Back crawl

movement with an approximately eighteen-inch depth of kick. The arms are also in alternate and continuous movement with no pause from the time of entry through the pulling stage, the lift and the swing through to re-entry.

Efficiency in the stroke depends on shoulder mobility and the entry point will be affected by this. The ideal entry can be found if the pupil's arm is straight, with the little finger entering the water first just wide of the shoulder line. The under water pull varies from pupil to pupil. There are in fact two ways of pulling. The straight-armed pull consists of shallow semi-circular movement just below the surface. The other type of pull starts with a straight entry. Then the elbow is bent and the arm is pulled to the shoulder line and pushed the remainder of the way to the thigh. Use the pull which seems most natural to the pupil.

Demonstrations and practices

The practices suggested here are progressive but they are only for *guidance*. How they are used will depend upon your pupil's ability. The whole stroke can be seen as the swimmer passes: the arm movement from the front and the leg movement from the rear.

Sculling should be practised lying horizontally on the back with or without the leg movement, but with the arms held at the sides. Push the water towards the feet, with the hands using a wrist movement only. Floats can be held on the chest with both hands, or extended beyond the head, or one float can be placed under each armpit. Before starting these practices make sure that the pupil can regain his feet.

Leg exercises

a   Push from the side with a float under each arm. Add the leg action which the teacher should check

b   Repeat a with the float on the chest

c   Repeat a with float extended beyond the head

d   Repeat a with hand-sculling

e   Get into a canoeing position stretched on the surface with the hands behind the back. Roll full circle, using only the legs and completing several revolutions

All these exercises should start with two or three yards' travel and increase with greater ability. Check that the pupil has a flat body position, correct head position, that his toes are just breaking the surface and that he has a correct leg action with flexible ankles.

Arm exercises

a   Put the toes under the rail and get into the back float position. Place the float either under one arm or with a bent elbow resting on it and do the arm movement with the free arm

b   Repeat a with the opposite arm

c   Put the toes under the rail and practise alternate arm movements without a float

d   Push from the side, adding arm movement for three or four yards but letting the legs trail

e   Push from the side, adding the leg movement and then the hand scull. After three or four yards commence the arm action but maintain teacher-controlled timing

f   Repeat e for a half to a full width, maintaining the teacher's control but building up a rhythm

g   Return to the practices for fault correction and then repeat exercise f, increasing the distance with greater efficiency

In all the above practices emphasis should be on a straight arm entry just wide of the shoulders and a continuous leg action involving movement at the thigh. No special practices for breathing are required in the back crawl. Emphasise that normal breathing should fit into a regular part of the stroke and check that no-one is holding his breath.

Points to watch for with new swimmers

General
a   Good body balance
b   Comfortable head position
c   No sitting in the water
d   No wriggling of the hips

Arms
a   Arms straight but not stretched or over-reaching themselves
b   Pausing at the thigh after the pull
c   Correct entry point, which is just wide of the shoulder
d   Hand position at entry with the little finger going in first
e   Wrist firm on the pull
f   Suitability of straight or bent arm pull for the particular pupil
g   Depth of pull approximately twelve inches

Legs
a   Action commencing in the hips
b   Legs close together
c   Strong even rhythm
d   Not too much bending in the knee
e   Strong upthrust as the lower leg pushes to the surface
f   Relaxed ankles with a slight turning in of the toes

The dolphin butterfly

Although the dolphin butterfly is not normally taught as a beginners' stroke I have included it in this chapter for continuity. This stroke needs a great deal of shoulder strength and physical stamina, together with a high degree of coordination. Even trained swimmers sometimes find it difficult to master the techniques, so it is not usually taught to beginners who are learning to swim for pleasure.

The dolphin butterfly is performed in the prone position. The propulsion is provided by the arms, which work together. The legs move up and down in a double crawl action. The breathing should be timed to take place as the arms pull beneath the body. It can be carried out by turning the head to the side, which helps to keep the body flat or by holding the head still as the shoulders rise on the pull. Breathing can be timed to occur either each time the arms pull, or every second time the arms pull, or at irregular intervals to suit the swimmer. The body should always be as flat as possible on the water.

Order of limb movement during the stroke

The butterfly is a comparatively new stroke in competitive swimming and has not yet reached its maximum efficiency as a racing stroke. Performance techniques are still largely in the experimental stage and there are differences of opinion about them. This means there is a wide variation in the way the movements are interpreted by swimmers and teachers. The teacher's views will depend on his personal feelings about the many factors involved, but the swimmer's will tend to depend on his physical and mental make-up. Unless you are teaching for competitive swimming these individual variations are irrelevant.

Features of the stroke

Put the legs together and relax the ankles. The movement should start in the hips and flow through the legs with a slight knee bend and a final flick through the feet. The arms working together are flung forward to enter the water slightly bent at the elbows, between the middle line of the body and the shoulder line. They pull immediately under the body to just beyond the hip line. Without pausing the arms are then lifted and flung forward for re-entry. Breathing is slotted in as the shoulders rise on the pull.

The arms enter the water with the hands pressing against it. The hips rise as the knees bend, so the thighs tend to slope downwards and the lower part of the leg upwards. As the arms pull under the body the legs straighten out to beat on the surface at the moment of pull, giving balance and propulsion to the movement. This movement is for the cycle of one leg beat to one arm movement. If you are using two leg beats the timing is

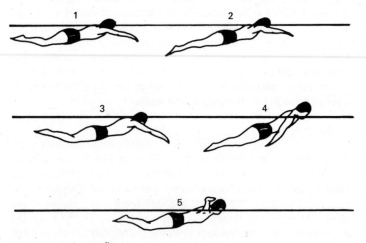

4   Dolphin butterfly

different. The first beat occurs as the arms enter and press against the water and the second takes place as the arms pull under the body. The teacher should encourage the pupil to use the leg beat which is most natural to him.

Demonstrations

The teacher should adapt the suggested exercises to suit the needs of his pupil or class. The dolphin butterfly stroke can be viewed as a whole from the side, the arm movement from the front and side, and the legs from behind the swimmer. It is essential for the teacher to realize that the stroke can be taught in several different ways. It can be approached as an adaptation from the breaststroke legs or arm movement, or as a new stroke. Use whichever method seems most suitable for your pupil. The following practices are for teaching the dolphin butterfly as a new stroke.

a   For railwork, grip the rail with the back of the hands to the wall and the elbows against it
b   For floatwork, hold the float in an extended position beyond the head
c   For canoeing, get into a horizontal position with the hands clasped behind the back and practise the leg movement only

Practices

Leg movements
a   Slowly practise the leg movements at the rail checking for a correct movement at a depth of eighteen inches
b   Hold on to the rail with the arms extended and repeat exercise a
c   Push off under water from the side, with the arms extended beyond the head and do two or three kicks. The teacher should check that this is being done correctly and then get the pupil to repeat the movement for four or five kicks
d   Push off from the side holding the float. Keep the head up and practise the leg kick for half a width
e   Repeat d holding the float but putting the face in the water. Lift the head to breathe. The pupil should aim to achieve a balanced flat position and a rhythmic movement
f   Repeat exercise e without using a float
g   Two pupils hold one float between them at arm's length. They kick their legs, trying to push their partner backwards. The teacher should check that they are performing the correct kick.
Arm movements
a   With the pupil standing with the water at chest level, the teacher can work on arm movements, breaking them down into their detailed components if necessary
b   Repeat a with the pupil controlling his own efforts. Slowly build this up until he is achieving a steady rhythm

c Push away from the side and do two arm pulls, letting the legs trail. The teacher should check the heaving action and make sure the pupil has a fast recovery to the re-entry point

d Repeat c doing four arm pulls and adding the breathing which is most natural to the pupil

e Push off from the side, then do the leg movement and two arm pulls. Put the head in and do not attempt to breathe. Repeat this several times adding to the number of strokes as the pupil's ability increases

f Repeat e adding the breathing method most natural to the pupil

g To test the heaving action and vary the lesson put a rubber ring attached to a rope round the pupil. Hold this taut against his arm action but do not pull on it

Points to watch for with new swimmers

General
a Good coordination
b Flat body position
c Relaxation
d Guard against excessive undulation

Arms
a Heaving action should be forwards and not upwards
b Fast unbroken arm action
c Entry point should not be too wide or too narrow
d Pulling line should be under or just outside the body line
e The elbows should be slightly bent on entry

Legs
a Strength of kick
b Legs together
c Depth of kick should be approximately eighteen inches
d Relaxed ankles
e Good upward movement of the legs
f Correct action starting in the hips and using a slight knee-bend

Breathing
a Is it suitable for your pupil?
b Is the side or frontal breathing suitable for him?
c Timing of the in-breath: early or late?

d   Suitability to the pupil of the breathing timing
e   Effect of breathing on the body position.

Adaptations from the breaststroke tend to give hybrid strokes. As the dolphin butterfly is a stroke in its own right, I feel that it is better to teach it as a separate stroke. It can also be taught with a glide between the cycles, but this is difficult for beginners because the whole purpose of the stroke is to achieve a continuous movement. To glide between cycles defeats the object, as the swimmer accelerates by pulling and then decelerates by gliding. The momentum which should be maintained by continuous action is lost.

The English backstroke

Due to the modern emphasis on the breaststroke, front and back crawl and butterfly, some of the older strokes are not widely taught. This means that although the pupil has better facilities at his disposal he is not experiencing the entire range of watermanship and also does not realise the sheer pleasure of doing some of the lesser known strokes. This is a pity, because some of them are important for survival and also enjoyable to do. The English backstroke is rarely taught, but it is worth the effort to teach this pleasant stroke.

Its main features are the distinctive action of the lower part of the legs during the kick, the high double arm recovery over the water, the shallow, semi-circular pull and the complete relaxation characteristic of the stroke. As in many of the older strokes, the English-backstroke swimmer has a choice of arm movements. The more accepted method is to take the arms out of the water on completion of the pull and swing them overhead ready to re-enter for the next pull. The Lancashire method, as it is called, allows the arms to remain underwater throughout the recovery phase up to the starting position of the pull.

Order of limb movement

To do the English backstroke the swimmer pushes off and at the same time his arms swing up and over to enter the water beyond the head while he turns his hands at the wrist ready to pull. The arms then sweep sideways in a semi-circular movement towards the thighs. The swimmer breathes out during the pull. The arms are now held at the side and the body glides through the water. As the speed of the glide decreases the legs kick together and the arms swing over the body ready for re-entry. The swimmer should breathe in at the highest point of the arm-swing.

The leg action is *not* a breaststroke kick performed on the back. The kick is made *from the knees* by the lower legs. There

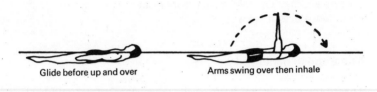

Glide before up and over   Arms swing over then inhale

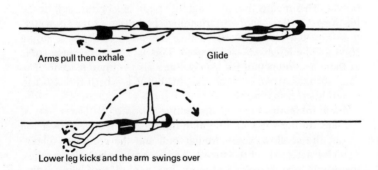

Arms pull then exhale   Glide

Lower leg kicks and the arm swings over

5   English backstroke

should be no movement in the thighs, which remain just beneath the surface and in line with the trunk. At the beginning of the movement the knees should part approximately six inches. The heels then swing out sideways so that the lower leg is taken to the limit of the knee joint. The feet then swing round and forward in a swirling motion until they reach the surface, when the ankles should be relaxed and the legs in line with the body. To repeat the movement the lower legs are dropped vertically from the knee joint and the movement is repeated. The kick must be correct, or the pupil will not make much progress with this stroke.

All demonstrations for this stroke are best viewed from above and behind the swimmer. The practices which have been suggested are for arm recovery out of the water. An initial trial of this exercise on land using a bench or the side of the bath may be helpful for the beginner.

Practices

Place the body in a horizontal position with the lower legs hanging vertically from the knee joint. The pupil can also try sculling in a back float position with the arms to the sides, pushing the water towards the feet and using the hands only.

Leg movements

a Demonstrate the leg action on land and in the water
b Practise the leg movement with the teacher's guidance if necessary
c Float in shallow water using a hand scull but without if possible. Practise the leg movement
d The teacher should let the pupil repeat exercise c by himself but check he is doing it properly
e Float in shallow water using a hand scull, but without aids if possible. Do the leg movement for a half or a full width while the teacher checks the balance and corrects the kick
f Repeat e and then use just the legs with the hands resting on the hips. The pupil should increase the distance he can swim as he becomes more proficient at the stroke
g Repeat f using just the legs, but varying the position of the arms to rest them on the hips, folded on the chest, or behind the head

Arm movements

a Push off lying on the back and glide with the arms beyond the head
b Repeat a but when the speed of the glide falls pull the arms to the thighs. The arms should be straight and at a depth of approximately six inches
c Repeat b and proceed to breathe out on the pull. Pause at the thighs, swing the arms over for re-entry and breathe in on the swing. Do two of the arm movements letting the legs trail. Repeat this until it is correct

Combining the skills
a   Push off and swing the arms over to enter the water. Pull on the arms and breathe out, pausing when the arms reach the thighs. Simultaneously kick the legs, swing the arms over and breathe in. Repeat these cycles several times
b   Return to the detailed practices to correct any faults
c   Repeat exercise a three or four times, gliding in the water and building up the distance covered

Points to watch for with new swimmers

General
a   Good co-ordination
b   Horizontal position
c   Good balance
d   Relaxed head position
Arms
a   Fast and relaxed upswing
b   The wrists turned ready to pull when the hands enter the water
c   Shallow pull to a depth of three to six inches
d   Straight arms with an even pull and no snatching
e   Pause at the sides to glide
f   The arms should enter beyond the head at shoulder width if possible
Legs
a   Correct kick using only the lower leg
b   Thighs in line with the trunk
c   Flexible ankles
d   Knees approximately six inches apart at the start of the kick
e   Legs hanging vertically at the start of the kick
f   Legs in line with the body at the end of the kick
The most difficult part of the English backstroke is making the leg kick coincide with the upswing of the arms and the timing of the breathing in at the highest point of the arm-swing. Make sure that the pupil's kick is well-established before he attempts the whole stroke, as the body mainly depends on this movement for propulsion when the arms are swung up and over. If there is no propulsion at this moment, the body will tend to submerge and disrupt the timing of the whole stroke.

The inverted breaststroke

Although the inverted breaststroke appears similar to the English backstroke, it is in fact totally different apart from being performed on the back. It is comfortable, free from breathing problems and can be very helpful in teaching the orthodox breaststroke leg movement. The inverted breaststroke is especially suitable for survival work.

The legs give propulsion and balance to the inverted breast-stroke. The arm movements can be performed either by hand-sculling or by drawing the hands up the sides to the armpits and then moving them sideways. They finally sweep in a shallow semi-circular movements towards the thighs and must be kept submerged throughout the movement. This is an extremely easy stroke for beginners to learn.

Order of limb movement during the stroke

Starting in the horizontal back float position the knees are drawn up *outside* the body line at the same time as the lower legs are dropped vertically from the knees. As they drop the

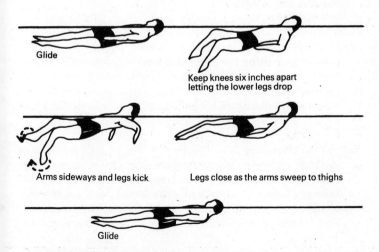

Glide

Keep knees six inches apart
letting the lower legs drop

Arms sideways and legs kick   Legs close as the arms sweep to thighs

Glide

6   Inverted breaststroke

arms are drawn up the sides of the body to the armpits and then extended sideways with the palms towards the feet. As the arms reach the sideways position, the legs kick and this is followed *immediately* by the arms sweeping to the thighs. The body is now in a glide position ready to repeat the stroke.

The legs should move fractionally before the arms in the stroke cycle. The leg kick is a normal breaststroke kick performed on the back.

Practices

The inverted breaststroke can best be seen from above and behind the swimmer.

Leg movements

a   Float on the back in shallow water with aids if required. Practise the leg kick with manual guidance if this seems necessary

b   Repeat exercise a with the teacher checking for a correct movement

c   Repeat b with hand-sculling. Build the distance up to four or five yards once the pupil is doing the movement properly

d   Repeat c while building rhythm and balance by doing first a half and then a full width

Arm movements

Demonstrate the arm movements on land and in the water

a   Push off from the side into a back float position with the legs trailing. Bring the arms to the sides and practise a slow arm movement under the teacher's control for one or two cycles. The teacher should check and correct the pupil's movements before repeating the exercise

b   Repeat a allowing free practice and building up to three or four cycles

Combining the skills

a   Push off into a back float position keeping the arms to the sides. Do two leg kicks with a hand scull. When the body is balanced before the third kick commences draw the arms to a sideways position and then do two full stroke movements. Check that this is correct, returning to the practices to cure any faults

b   Push off and practise the full stroke for half a width building up the distance with increasing efficiency

Points to watch for with new swimmers

General
a   Good balance
b   Body just beneath the surface with slight incline from shoulders to feet
c   Comfortable head position
Legs
a   Knees kept below the surface
b   Good swirling action in the lower leg
c   Full ankle flexibility in the final kick
Arms
a   Depth of pull should be between six and nine inches
b   Straight and even arm pull from the shoulder line
c   Palms turned to the line of the pull

The side-stroke

The relaxing side-stroke can be used over great distances so it is well suited for survival and life-saving work. It is performed on the side with the arms working alternately. One should pull down the front of the body as the other pulls immediately under it. The legs lie parallel just below the surface and perform a simple scissor movement, timed to kick as the upper arms pulls and to recover as the lower one does. There are few breathing problems with this stroke as the face is not submerged. The arm movement can be performed with an underwater or over the water recovery. The type of upper arm pull will vary with the pupil and can be a straight-armed semi-sircular sweep to the thigh, or a pull to the chest line followed by a push for the remainder of the distance to the thigh.

Order of limb movement during the stroke

The swimmer pushes off with his arms beyond his head. One arm pulls the body on to the swimming side, so this should be a right arm pull if he is going to swim on the left side and vice versa. After the initial arm pull the upper arm slides along the body to an extended position, at the same time as the lower arm pulls under the body to the chest level *from* an extended position. The legs open forwards and backwards to kick. As the lower arm returns to the extended position the upper arm starts pulling and the legs kick. All the limbs should be kept underwater throughout the stroke.

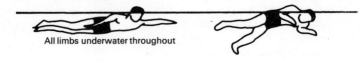

All limbs underwater throughout

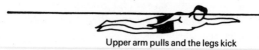

Upper arm pulls and the legs kick

7   Side-stroke

Demonstrations and practices

The side-stroke leg movement can best be viewed from above and behind the swimmer. The arm movement and the stroke as a whole should be seen from the swimmer's stroking side. Use a float to practise:

a   Upper arm movement. The lower arm is extended beyond the head with the palm on the float
b   Lower arm movement. The upper arm is bent at the elbows and has the hand resting on the float at the chest line
c   Leg kick movement. The lower arm rests on the float as in a, while the upper arm rests along the side of the body.

To demonstrate the arm movement stand sideways so the surface view can be seen by the class. The appropriate lower arm should be extended beyond the head. To do the leg practice at the rail one hand grasps it and the palm of the lower arm rests against the wall with the body on the swimming side.

Practices with all limbs under water

Leg movement
a   Demonstrate the leg movement in the water

b   Practise the leg kick

c   Holding a float push off and turn on to the swimming side. The teacher should check that this is being done correctly

d   Using a float increase the distance as the kick becomes more effective. The teacher should check that the movement is from the hip. The ankles should be flexible during the kick and it should end with the legs together

Arm movement

a   Demonstrate the movement on land and in the water

b   Stand with the water up to chest level. Put the legs apart and bend to the swimming side. Practise the upper arm pull first, then the lower arm pull, and finally combine and time alternate pulls

c   Holding a float in shallow water, practise the upper arm pull allowing the legs to trail

d   Repeat exercise c while practising the lower arm pull

Breathing

As the face is clear breathing presents few problems. The swimmer normally breathes in as the upper arm pulls, and out as it recovers.

a   Push off from the side with the legs trailing and do one pull to the swimming side. Then do the arm stroke for two or three cycles with breathing. The teacher should check the pupil's timing and repeat this exercise until he can do it properly

Combining the skills

a   Push off, repeating the above exercises for the arm movement and breathing and adding the leg movement as the upper arm pulls for one or two cycles

b   Return to specific practices to correct faults

c   Build up the distance with increasing efficiency

Side-stroke with over the water recovery

The only difference between side-strokes with under and over the water recovery is that in the latter the upper arm is taken out of the water at the thigh line for a re-entry beyond the head. All the other movements are the same as for under water recovery, but the body tends to roll more when the swimmer uses over the water recovery.

38

Points to watch for with new swimmers

General
a   Good balance for both methods
b   Body in line
c   Relaxation
d   Good rhythm
Arm movement: under water recovery
a   Coordination and timing
b   Even pulling
c   Direction of the pull
d   Arm movements close to the body
e   Limbs under water throughout
Arm movement: over the water recovery
a   The arm should not be too high as this causes the swimmer to turn over
b   No swinging out of the arm
c   Relaxed arm slightly bent for re-entry
d   No digging in deep on entry
Legs
a   Correct kick starting in the hips and flowing through the legs
b   No excessive knee bend
c   Rhythm
d   Legs together in line with the body after the kick
e   Good ankle flexibility
f   No hip twist when kicking
Breathing
a   No turning the head around to breathe
b   Not too much head lift
c   Head comfortable throughout with one ear submerged
d   Breathe in *one* part of the stroke cycle

Although the side-stroke movements may sound a little complicated, it is in fact quite an easy stroke to learn. The arm movements are the most difficult for beginners but a good demonstration and careful attention to basic practices should prove sufficient to enable the average pupil to learn the stroke.

Life-saving backstroke

The life-saving backstroke is an essential skill in life-saving and personal survival work. It is easy to learn and strongly recommended to the teacher. The stroke is performed on the back with the main propulsion coming from the leg action. It can be performed in several different ways, each of which is described below but in *all* methods it is important to keep the knees below the surface of the water. The arms can either perform a sculling action or move sideways.

Order of limb movement during the stroke

Float on the back with the head resting comfortably on the water. The arms can be placed on the hips, folded on the chest, or clasped behind the head. Allow the legs to drop vertically from the knee-joints, which should be about six inches apart. Swing the lower legs outwards to the full extent of the knee-joints and then forward again in a vigorous circular movement with full ankle flexibility, until they come together in line with the body. The thighs are kept as still as possible and in line with the body during the movement. This is the basic leg movement, to which will be added the two possible arm movements.

First practise adding hand sculling at the sides. For this the hands move from the wrists performing figure-of-eight movements and pushing the water towards the feet.

The other arm movement involves putting the arms sideways so that they can pull when the legs kick. To do this successfully both movements *must* occur simultaneously. As the lower legs drop vertically, the arms are taken upwards along the thighs to the hip level. As the knees bend to start the kick, the elbows bend outwards and then straighten to take the arms sideways at a thirty-degree angle from the body. When the legs sweep forward to complete the kick, the arms are also swept forward to the thighs. The body is now in a glide position ready to repeat the movement.

Demonstrations and practices

The pupil should see a demonstration of life-saving backstroke from above and behind the swimmer.

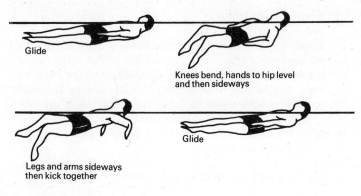

Glide

Knees bend, hands to hip level
and then sideways

Legs and arms sideways
then kick together

Glide

8 Life-saving backstroke

Method 1

a   Demonstrate the stroke on land using a bench or the side of the bath. The pupil lies horizontally on his back so that the legs are free to drop vertically in practising the stroke
b   Repeat exercise a in the water
c   Repeat a in shallow water using aids if required. Check the movement of the legs
d   Repeat c without aids if possible. Start from the back float position and make the arm movement optional to start with. Practise the leg kicks until the pupil can do several strokes

Method 2

a   Stand up in water up to chest level. Practise the hand scull under the teacher's supervision
b   In shallow water push off into a back float; let the legs trail and practise the scull

Combine the skills

Push off from the side into the back float. Practise the leg kick for two or three yards, then add the scull. The teacher should check that the leg movement and the balance are correct. If the head is properly positioned the swimmer is able to breathe normally

Method 3

a   Demonstrate the arm movement standing on the side
b   Get the pupil in shallow water, doing a back float with aids

if required. Let the legs trail and practise the arm movement under the teacher's control

c   Repeat b under individual control with the teacher checking the movement

d   Standing in water at chest level and using aids if they seem necessary, slowly practise the full stroke movement. Build up the rhythm and distance with increasing efficiency

Points to watch for with new swimmers

Method 1
a   No sitting in the water
b   Good balance
c   Vigorous and even kick
d   Circular movement of the lower legs
e   Knees below the surface
f   Flexible ankles
g   Glide between the kicks
h   Steady rhythm
i   Legs in line with the body after the kick
j   Arms in a comfortable position

Method 2
a   No flapping at the wrists
b   Direction of the hand-push
c   Arms to the side and relaxed
d   Hands working together for good balance

Method 3
a   Timing of movements
b   All limbs under water
c   All limbs working together simultaneously
d   Even kick and push with no snatching
e   Calm arm movements to a sideways position
f   Good balance
g   No lifting of the head

The surface arm backstroke

The surface arm backstroke brings us into the field of hydrotherapy or swimming for handicapped pupils. I have included a chapter on the subject for guidance for those who, although they have no experience, may have to teach such a pupil. This stroke is performed on the back with all the limbs submerged. Propulsion comes firstly from the leg kick which is followed by a glide and secondly from the arm pull which is also followed by a glide. There should be no breathing problems with this stroke, as the face is clear of the water.

Starting from an initial horizontal back float position, the arms are drawn along the body until they reach the top of the head. At the same time the lower legs are dropped vertically as the knees part. While the legs move sideways the arms continue their movement to their fullest extension beyond the head. At this point the legs kick coming together with the body in the glide position. As the speed of the glide slows down, the arms sweep round in a shallow semi-circular movement to the thighs, with the legs remaining still. The body is thus again in a glide position ready to repeat the stroke cycle.

Demonstrations and practices

Arrange demonstrations to show the surface arm backstroke from above and behind the swimmer. The arm movement can be

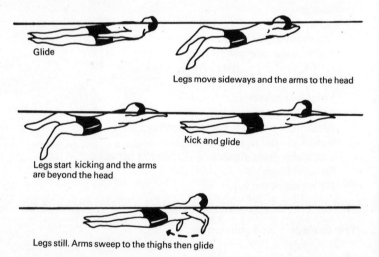

Glide

Legs move sideways and the arms to the head

Legs start kicking and the arms are beyond the head

Kick and glide

Legs still. Arms sweep to the thighs then glide

9   Surface arm backstroke

seen from above and directly in front and the leg action from the rear. If your pupil is disabled the aids he requires will depend on the nature of his disability and what is available. You should get medical advice about the pupil's suitability for water-work. The leg movement is identical to the life-saving backstroke leg movement, which has already been described.

a   Demonstrate the arm movement on land and in the water

b   Get the pupil in shallow water supported by aids. In a back float position practise the arm movement along the sides to the head position and turning the palms with the fingers pointing beyond the head. Then extend the arms beyond the head with the palms facing outwards

c   Do a back float in shallow water supported by aids. Practise the first part of the arm movement with the knees parting and the lower legs dropping to a vertical position

d   Repeat c, adding the second part of the arm movement so that, as the arms stretch above the head, the legs commence a sideways movement. The lower legs kick until the legs are in line with the body, then the swimmer glides

e   Repeat d up to the glide, then add a shallow arm sweep from beyond the head to the thighs

f   Combine the skills to do the whole stroke using aids if necessary. Do half a width and then a width, building up a steady rhythm. The teacher should check that the movements and timing are correct

Points to watch for with new swimmers

General
a   Relaxation
b   As horizontal a position as possible
c   Good balance
d   Timing is vitally important to a well-balanced stroke
e   No bending or sitting in the water

Arm movements
a   Limbs kept under water
b   Elbows square to the water when moving from the thighs to beyond the head
c   Quiet movements
d   Palms turned to the line of the pull
e   Shallow semi-circular pull from three to six inches deep
f   Straight and even arm pull

Leg movements
a   Knees not too far apart to start the kick
b   Strong even kick with a full lower leg swirl
c   Good ankle flexibility
d   Legs not too low in the water when gliding after the kick

4

Starts

Starting belongs to competitive swimming, but I have included it because it enhances the pupil's watermanship. It is also a balancing activity for lessons and can be great fun to learn. The start is vital for competitive swimming and has additional refinements for each stroke. The full details of these will be given here to assist anyone who wishes to learn the techniques.

The front crawl start

The initial stance for the front crawl start is with the feet approximately a hip-width apart, forming a firm base. The toes should be curled over the edge and the knees slightly bent. The trunk is curved over in a comfortable position and the head well-balanced without any strain on the neck muscles. The eyes should be fixed on a point two or three yards ahead on the surface. The arms either hang loosely from the shoulders or are held slightly backwards, but they are always relaxed. The whole stance should be as relaxed as possible with maximum alertness.

Order of limb movement during the start

The following sequence is continuous with no pause in *any* phase. When the swimmer is told to take his mark, his stance becomes firm but not tense, his mind should be very alert and his body poised, balanced and perfectly still. When he hears the signal his body weight moves forward over the balls of his feet. The arms move backwards and are *immediately* flung forward in line with the trunk with the head between them. At the same time as the arms are brought back the knees bend. When the arms are flung forward the legs straighten vigorously against the side. As this contact with the side is lost the body should be in one unbroken line from the fingertips to the ends of the toes. This stretched position is held throughout the time in the air and under water. When the swimmer's speed falls away, the leg kick

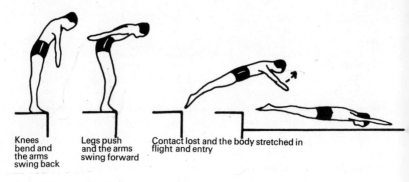

Knees bend and the arms swing back

Legs push and the arms swing forward

Contact lost and the body stretched in flight and entry

10   Starts

commences with one arm pull to bring the body to the surface. The depth of the dive for the front crawl should be about eighteen inches.

Demonstrations and practices

Your pupil will best be able to see demonstrations of this start, particularly the take-off, from a sideways angle. The pick-up of the arm movement can be seen from the front and the pick-up of the leg kick from behind the swimmer.

a   Demonstrate the whole skill up to when the pupil swims out
b   Demonstrate the movements involved on land. Point out the positions of the feet, trunk, head and arms, the knee bend and the focal point for the eyes. Get your pupil to assume positions then check them and correct any faults he may have
c   Demonstrate the take-off on land emphasizing firstly alertness after the preliminary command and secondly a shifting of the weight to the balls of the feet. The pupil's partner should give him shoulder support from the front. The shoulders move forward, the arms swing back and knees bend.
d   Repeat c with a slow leg-stretch and a forward arm-swing. The teacher should check the pupil's timing and get him to repeat this exercise three or four times, coordinating the movements but still using partner support

e   Practise the full skill of take-off with the teacher checking the timing, coordination and angle of the body

f   Practise the full skill with the teacher checking the angle of entry, depth and stroke pick-up

A towel can be held round the pupil's chest from the rear to support him in these practices.

Points to watch for with learners

a   Firm base for take-off
b   Feet about the width of the hips apart but not too angled
c   Good head position with no strain on the neck muscles
d   Relaxed shoulders
e   Hips over the feet
f   No leaning forward as this will upset the pupil's balance
g   Not too much bending in the knees
h   Feet flat on the side of the bath until the start signal, as this prevents strain
i   Maximum alertness without tensing after the preliminary command
j   Coordination on take-off
k   Thrust outwards *not* upwards
l   Body straight on take-off with no bottom or head lift
m   Angle of entry should not be too deep or shallow
n   Correct point for the leg pick-up
o   Correct point for the arm pull to the surface
p   Smooth transition to the full stroke when swimming out

The breaststroke start

The stance and take-off for the breaststroke start is the same as for the front crawl, except that the angle of entry is steeper and the start reaches a depth of two to two and a half feet. As the glide speed falls away the swimmer does one full breaststroke arm movement pulling straight through to the thighs. This is followed *immediately* by a leg kick to bring the body to the surface ready to swim out on the full stroke. The head must break the surface before the second stroke is taken. The teacher should check the same details as for the front crawl start. Also look for a steeper take-off angle and depth, a full double arm pull under water and a leg kick to the surface.

The dolphin butterfly start

The correct stance and depth for the dolphin butterfly start are the same as for the breaststroke start. The leg kick commences as the speed of the dive falls and a double arm pull under the body brings it to the surface. This is *immediately* followed by an arm recovery *over* the water to the entry point for the second stroke. The head must break the surface before the second stroke is taken.

The points to watch for with beginners are the same as for the breaststroke. In addition the teacher should check the speed on the leg pick-up, the double arm pull under the body with an immediate recovery over the water, and that there is no undue arching of the back in the underwater pull.

The backstroke start

The backstroke start is made in the water. The body is held in a loose tuck position with the hands gripping the bar or starting-block handles and the feet resting on the wall under the surface. The position should be held without straining the neck, arm or shoulder muscles and with eyes fixed on the wall immediately in front of the pupil. The order of limb movements during the start should be continuous and the swimmer should not pause in any phase. When the 'take your marks' signal is heard, the stance becomes firm but not tense and the body is pulled slightly in to the wall in a tightened tuck, with the shoulders raised just above the surface. The mind should be as alert as possible. The position of the feet should provide a firm base for the leg thrust with the balls of the feet against the wall, so that there is complete immobility. When the 'go' signal is given the feet thrust vigorously against the wall with a fast leg extension. At the same time the arms are flung upwards and backwards with the head tucked between them. The back must be arched high with the body stretched to bring it clear of the water. As the body strikes the water either partially or wholly submerged, the legs start to kick. One arm pull brings the body to the surface and the swimmer immediately starts to swim out on a full stroke. The depth of the dive for this start is very shallow, usually only about twelve inches, and some swimmers do not fully submerge on the start at all. When the body is fully submerged, one arm pull will bring it to the surface and there will be immediate leg and arm stroke pick-ups. The degree of clearance above the water is important for a good backstroke start. The swimmer should push off *backwards and upwards*.

Practices for beginners

a Demonstrate in the water the full start, stance and the take-off.
b Get into the tuck position on land using a pole or gripping a partner's hands. The feet are against the wall or the partner's front lower legs. Check the head and shoulder positions and the arm width
c Repeat b in the water. The teacher should check the foot movement under water
d Repeat c, practising the arm release and the upswing with the partial leg push. A shirt or singlet will reduce the pain of the water-sting at this stage.
e Repeat c, practising the leg thrust with the arched back and the arms to the sides
f Combine d and e into a full movement and repeat this three or four times
g Repeat f, adding the leg and arm pick-ups and swimming out

Points to watch for with learners

a Comfortable unstrained tuck position
b Head position not straining the neck muscles
c Alertness and making the tuck firm on the preliminary command
d Firm but relaxed grip in the hand-hold
e Foot position on the wall for maximum thrust
f Fast leg extension
g Body stretch and arch on take-off
h Head position on take-off

i   Co-ordination of complete movement
j   Arm position on take-off
k   No buckling on entry
l   Depth of the start
m   Smooth breaking into the full stroke

Summary

Starting is an art in itself for which perfect balance and coordination are essential. These will not come until the mind is fully alert on the preliminary command and the reflexes are well-practised. All starts should be timed with a stopwatch to test their efficiency. They can be timed from the starting signal to the moment of surfacing, or to the first full stroke cycle or even to a given distance. This can be marked by holding a pole at the desired distance from the take-off point and stopping the watch as the swimmer comes in line with it. When you are teaching starts to non-competitive swimmers make sure you have a clear idea of the standard you wish to attain.

5

Turns

The art of turning, together with starts, belongs to competitive
swimming, but I have included it in this volume because it is
enjoyable and useful to learn. Each turn has its particular
refinements in relation to different strokes. This detail may not
be required in teaching for recreational purposes, but all the
turns will be described in detail to enable any pupil who is
interested to learn all the techniques.

The breaststroke pivot turn
The breaststroke pivot turn is the simplest of the turns, although
it is rarely done correctly. Most swimmers heave themselves
upwards from the water but this is wasteful and exhausting. The
turn should be perfectly timed and executed with the minimum
of body lift.

Order of limb movement during the turn

Swim in to the wall at a good speed, assisting the final reach
with a strong leg kick. The palms touch the wall together on the
same level. The elbows bend to bring the body close to the wall
in the tuck position with the lower legs to the bottom. Swivel the
body either to the right or left, whichever is most natural, with
the assistance of a shoulder twist. The head rises slightly and
then the body is allowed to sink. The feet are placed against the
wall with the knees bent. The arms are bent with the hands
slightly beyond the head. The legs are vigorously extended so
that the body is propelled in an upward glide. As this speed falls
away one double arm pull is made through to the thighs,
followed immediately by one leg kick to bring the body to the
surface. Then start the full stroke and swim out rapidly.

Demonstrations and practices

See that this turn is demonstrated so that your pupil can see it

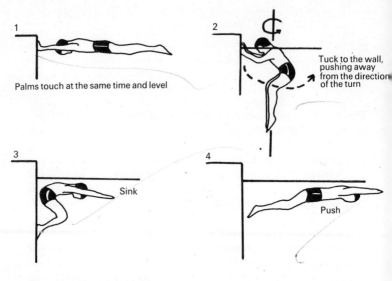

Palms touch at the same time and level

Tuck to the wall, pushing away from the direction of the turn

Sink

Push

11 Breaststroke pivot turn

from the front and above. The push-off and swimming out should also be seen from behind the swimmer. Divide the turn into three parts: the swim-in and touch, the tuck and swivel, and the push-off and swim-out.

a   Demonstrate the turn

b   Do a fast swim in, put the palms against the wall so that they touch together on the same level

c   Repeat b, bending the elbows and tucking the body close to the wall

d   Combine b and c adding the push and the swivel movement to the natural turning side. The shoulder twist should assist with the swivel

e   Combine and repeat exercises b, c and d until they are correct

f   Get into a starting position tucked to the wall and then push, swivel and raise the head slightly before allowing the body to sink

g   Start from a position treading water close to the wall but facing outwards. Practise the body sink and tuck with the feet to the wall. Push away, coordinate the sink and then push off on the front, slowly at first

h   Combine all the practices into the full skill, building up speed as efficiency increases. Add the break into the full stroke and swim out rapidly

Points to watch for with learners

a   Fast swim-in
b   Judgement of distance to the wall
c   *Never* glide to the wall, but *always* kick in to it
d   Put the palms to the wall at the same time and on the same level
e   Swivel to the natural side
f   Give a good shoulder twist to assist the hand as it pushes to swivel
g   No twisting off the wall as the body must be on the front for the push-off
h   The head rises for breath as the palms touch
i   Quick body sink
j   Do not use the rail to heave the body upwards
k   Feet flat against the wall for the push through the toes
l   Upward glide after the push-off
m   One full stroke to the thighs under water
n   One leg kick to drive the body to the surface
o   Swim-out rapidly

The dolphin butterfly pivot turn
The dolphin butterfly pivot turn is like the breaststroke turn except that in the underwater phase after pushing off from the wall, one double arm pull is taken under the body and the arms are immediately recovered over the water for re-entry. The leg kick should start immediately after the push-off.

The backstroke turns

There are three recognised turns used effectively for the back-stroke: the spin turn with the head out of the water, the spin turn with the head in the water and the back-somersault turn.

The backstroke spin with the head out turn

Order of limb movement during the turn

The pupil swims rapidly and while still on his back reaches to touch the wall. The body immediately tucks, swivels with the free hand assisting by sculling under the body, and sinks to the neck-level as the feet touch the wall. The body is now in a tucked position with one hand just above the head palm-

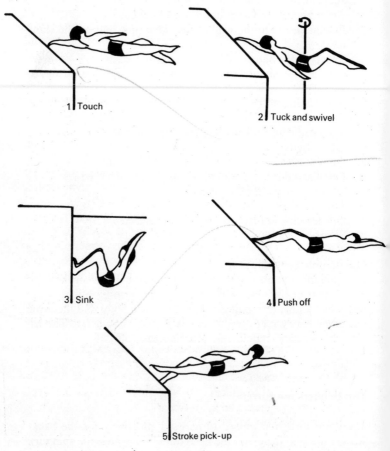

1 Touch

2 Tuck and swivel

3 Sink

4 Push off

5 Stroke pick-up

12   Backstroke spin head out turn

uppermost and the elbows bent. The legs extend vigorously and the body is stretched. The leg beat starts as soon as the legs have been straightened. One arm pull brings the body fully to the surface to swim out fast on a full stroke.

Demonstrations and practices

Demonstrations for this turn should be divided into three phases: the swim in and touch, the tuck, swivel and scull, and the sink and push-off. The whole turn and especially the swim in and touch should be viewed by the pupil from above and in front of the swimmer. The swivel and scull can be seen from the side and above, and the final sink and push-off from behind and above him.

a   Demonstrate the turn on land by sitting in a tucked position. Put the back to the wall and raise the palms of the touching hand to it. If the swimmer is spinning to the left, he should put the right hand to the wall with his fingers in the direction of the spin, and vice versa

b   Practise exercise a on land, simulating the spin by turning manually until the feet are against the wall

c   Let your pupil practise spinning by himself in the water. Sit in a tucked position and spin the body with a combination of hand sculling and shoulder twist

d   Get in the water close to the wall, from a tucked position spin half a turn and place the feet against the wall

e   Swim in slowly to touch the side. Tuck and then spin for a half-turn ending with the feet on the wall. Repeat this exercise, building up speed with efficiency and with the teacher checking all phases of the turn

f   Get into a start position tucked and facing the side of the bath. Practise the sink to the neck level only and placing the feet against the wall

g   Repeat f, placing the hands above the head with the palms upwards and the elbows bent, push off slowly and repeat this to build up speed

h   Combine all the practices in a full turn as far as the push-off. The teacher should check for faults

i   Return to the practices for fault correction

j   Practise the full turn from swimming-in to the stroke pick-up when the pupil swims out

Points to watch for with learners

a   Fast swim-in on the back
b   Judgement of distance to the wall
c   Palm to the wall with the fingers pointing in the direction of the spin
d   Free hand-sculling beneath the body to assist the spin
e   Shoulder twist to assist the spin
f   Spin to the natural side
g   Quick sink to the neck level only
h   Good tuck close to the wall
i   Feet flat to the wall to prevent skidding
j   Hands above the head immediately after the spin with the elbows bent and the palms upwards
k   Vigorous leg extension and final push through the toes
l   Good leg beat pick-up and one arm pull to the surface, followed by full stroke pick-up
m   General coordination of the turn
n   Fast swim-out

The backstroke spin with the head under turn
The spin turn with the head under water is a more complicated turn requiring good coordination and practice. You should teach the turn with the head out *first* as it will make it easier to teach it with the head under. Ensure that all the basic techniques are mastered before proceeding to the full turn.

Order of limb movements during the turn

After a fast swim-in the swimmer should touch the side while still on his back. The touching arm bends, the legs tuck up and the knees are pulled out of the water and over the shoulder of the touching arm. Simultaneously the body spins a half turn to bring the feet to the wall, the head drops backwards and the body sinks. From the touch to the spin and dropping of the head the free hand completes its pull and then assists the spin by a sculling action. The body is now in a tucked position with the feet to the wall, the arms above the head, the elbows bent and the palms uppermost. Push off with a fast leg extension. After the leg beat pick-up and one arm pull to bring the body to the surface, there is a fast swim-out on the full stroke.

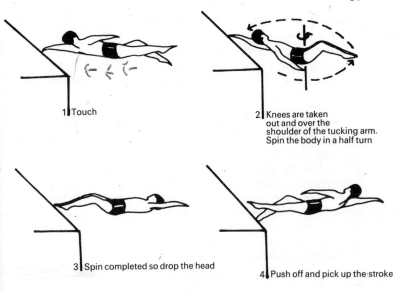

1 Touch

2 Knees are taken out and over the shoulder of the tucking arm. Spin the body in a half turn

3 Spin completed so drop the head

4 Push off and pick up the stroke

13   Backstroke spin head under turn

Demonstrations

a   Swim in, touch and pull the knees over (seen from in front and above)
b   Pull the knees over, spin and tuck with the feet to the wall (visible from above)
c   The head drops, the tuck and the arm position for the push-off (visible from above)
d   Push-off and swim-out (seen from the rear)
e   Complete turn (most easily seen from behind and above the swimmer)

If spinning left put the right hand to the wall with the fingers in the direction of the spin and vice versa

Practices

a   Demonstrate the turn in the water
b   In the water get into the tuck position, sculling with the hands and then practise simple spins with the head dropping

c   Free practice repeating exercise b but also putting the knees over and sinking

d   Swim in slowly then repeat exercise c at the side with the touch and the free arm scull

e   Swim in slowly then repeat exercise d at the side with the touch and the free arm scull

f   Faster swim in and then repeat e to bring the feet to the wall. The body should be tucked ready for the push-off

g   Combine the skills. Swim in, touch, pull the knees over the head, drop and then spin

h   Practise the complete turn from the swim-in to the push-off, adding the leg and arm pick-ups to a full fast stroke

Points to watch for with learners

a   Fast swim-in
b   Judgement of the distance to the wall
c   Palm to the wall and fingers in the direction of the spin
d   Free hand sculling to assist the spin
e   Knees at an angle over the touching arm's shoulder
f   Shoulder-assisted twist
g   Head-drop timing in the spin movement
h   Coordination of the tuck, movement of the knees being pulled over, the head drop and the sink
i   Good tuck for the push-off with the feet flat to the wall to prevent skidding
j   Arm and head positions in the push-off
k   Fast leg extension pushing out through the toes
l   Fast leg pick-up after the push-off
m   Smooth full stroke pick-up for a fast swim-out

The backstroke back-somersault turn
The backstroke back-somersault turn is not a simple back-somersault. It is a twisting back-somersault which enables the swimmer to come out of the the turn on his back ready for the push-off.

Order of limb movement during the turn

Swim in rapidly and then touch while still on the back with the palms to the wall and the fingers pointed downwards. The head drops back on the touch while the knees tuck up and are pulled straight over the body. When the head is at its lowest point and the feet are at their highest point, the body is twisted, still tucked to bring the feet to the wall. The body sinks and the push-off and swim-out are as previously described for the other backstroke turns. The body twist in the tucked position is assisted by the free hand sculling beneath the body.

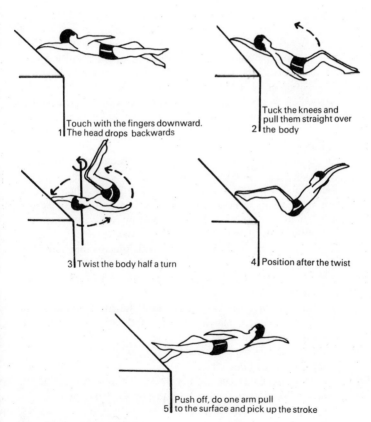

1 Touch with the fingers downward. The head drops backwards

2 Tuck the knees and pull them straight over the body

3 Twist the body half a turn

4 Position after the twist

5 Push off, do one arm pull to the surface and pick up the stroke

14   Back-somersault turn

Demonstrations

Arrange that this turn is demonstrated in four parts:

a Swim in, touch and tuck over (in front and above)
b Repeat a, adding the twist, put the feet to the wall and sink (in front and above)
c Push-off position under water and actual push-off (behind and to the side of the swimmer)
d The complete turn, first slowly and then at speed (in front, above and from behind)

Practices

a Demonstrate the turn in the water
b Get in shallow water and practise back-somersaulting to a standing position either with a push from the side or doing free somersaults. The head should be kept well back
c In shallow water practise the above exercise. Repeat it and add the twist with hand-sculling to assist the movement to a standing position. The pupil should finish the exercise facing the opposite side of the bath
d Swim in slowly, touch and tuck. The teacher should check the position of the hand on the wall
e Swim in slowly, touch and tuck. Add the twist when the feet are in a vertical position. The teacher should check the movement at the moment of twisting and see that the swimmer is hand-sculling beneath the body.
f Repeat exercise e, pushing hard with the turning hand on the wall to assist the somersault. Bring the feet to the wall with the body tucked. Repeat this with a faster swim-in as efficiency increases
g Repeat f adding the body sink and the push-off position. The teacher should check that the hands are in an overhead position for the push-off
h Combine the skills into the full turn with a slow swim-in. Check for any faults
i Return to the practices for any necessary fault correction
j Swim in fast and do a complete turn up to stroke pick-up

Points to watch for with learners

a Fast swim-in on the back

b   Palm to the wall on the touch with the fingers downwards
c   Fast head-drop on the touch
d   Tight tuck for the somersault
e   Feet come straight over the body, not at an angle
f   Shoulder twist to assist in the half-turn
g   Hand-scull beneath the body to assist the twist
h   Feet flat to the wall and push out through the toes
i   Quick sink as the feet touch the wall
j   Arm position for the push-off
k   Vigorous leg extension in the push-off
l   Fast leg beat pick-up after the push-off
m   One arm pull to bring the body to the surface
n   Smooth break into the full stroke
o   Overall coordination and timing of the turn

Free-style turns

The most popular freestyle turns in current use are the grab or throwaway turn and the tumble turn, which can be done with either the arm or the head leading the turn. These three turns will be described in detail together with suggested demonstrations and practices for the beginner.

The grab turn

Order of limb movements during the turn

The swimmer does a fast swim-in and his leading hand grasps the rail or the scum channel. The body is tucked and drawn to the wall and then immediately forcibly pushed away from the direction of the turn by the combination of the shoulder twisting and the hand pushing. The body, which is still in a tucked position, sinks and as it does so the grasping hand is thrown over to join the free hand beyond the head, ready for the push-off. The legs extend vigorously against the wall. The leg beat is picked up as the swimmer's speed falls away. One arm pull brings the body to the surface ready for the full stroke swim-out. Many swimmers grasp the rail or channel with both hands to turn, but this tends to break the swimming-in rhythm and should be avoided. Practise turning using alternate hands, concentrating first on the pupil's natural side.

Demonstrations and practices

Demonstrations for this turn are best given in two parts. The swim-in with the grab of the leading arm, the tuck and the forcible turn are best seen from in front and above. The throwing-over of the free hand, sinking into the push-off position and the push-off itself can best be seen from behind and above the swimmer.

a Demonstrate the full turn in the water
b Swim in slowly, grasp the rail and tuck the body
c Repeat exercise b, forcing the body round and pushing *away* from the direction of the turn. Twist the shoulder in the direction of the turn
d Repeat c, adding the free arm throw-over, the sinking movement and placing the tucked feet to the wall
e Start with the body tucked and the back to the wall. Practise the tuck, sink and push-off
f Combine the skills into the full turn. Do this slowly at first but building up speed with efficiency. The teacher should check for faults at this stage
g Return to the basic movements for fault correction
h Practise the complete turn from the swim-in to the swim-out on the full stroke

Points to watch for with learners

a Fast swim-in
b Judgement of the distance to the rail or channel
c Fast tuck to the wall as the elbow bends and the hand seizes the rail
d Direction of the hand-push and the shoulder-twist in the turn
e Fast free arm throw-over on the tuck and the sink
f Feet flat against the wall to prevent skidding
g Head position after the sink should not be too far back
h Body position for the push-off should be in line with the feet as this prevents skidding
i Fast leg extension in the push-off
j Overall coordination and timing of the turn

The tumble turn with the arm leading

Order of limb movements during the turn

After a fast swim-in the leading arm reaches and *immediately* pulls hard under the body. Simultaneously the head is forced down and the body tucks tight. The body then somersaults with the feet to the wall. As the legs extend vigorously the body stretches to push off and a shoulder twist brings it once more on to the breast for the upward glide. It is important that the twist is timed to take place as the legs extend. As the push-off speed falls away, the leg beat is picked up and one arm pull brings the swimmer to the surface ready for a fast full stroke swim-out.

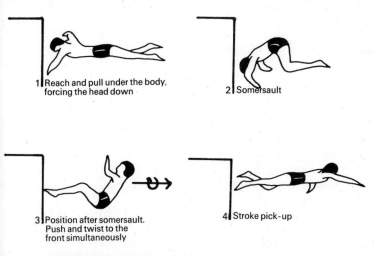

1 Reach and pull under the body, forcing the head down

2 Somersault

3 Position after somersault. Push and twist to the front simultaneously

4 Stroke pick-up

15   Tumble-turn arm leading

Demonstrations and practices

Arrange demonstrations for this turn in two parts. The fast swim-in, somersault and placing of the feet against the wall can be seen from in front and above. The push-off, twist, leg and arm pick-up and full stroke swim-out are best viewed from the rear.

64

a   Demonstrate the full turn in the water
b   Push from the side in shallow water and have free somer-saulting practice to a standing position with one arm pull under the body (seen from behind and above)
c   Free swimming and then repeat b to a standing position
d   Swim in slowly, reach for the side, and then somersault with the feet to the wall. Repeat this exercise three or four times, building up the speed of the swim-in and the somersault as the technique is mastered
e   Get in a starting position and grasp the bar with the body tucked. Practise the sink, push-off and twist, repeating the movements until they are correct and the twist is properly timed
f   Combine all the skills to do a complete turn. This should be done slowly at first but building up the pupil's speed with greater efficiency

Points to watch for with learners

a   Fast swim-in
b   Strong leading arm pull under the body
c   Head *must* be forced down as the arm pulls under the body
d   Tight tuck in to the somersault
e   Somersault must be square to the wall and not anticipate the twist
f   Feet firmly against the wall and pushing out with the toes
g   Timing of the push and the twist
h   Upward glide from the push-off
i   The timing of the leg action pick-up and the arm-pull to the surface
j   Smooth breaking into the full stroke swim-out
k   Judgement of the distance to the wall is *most important*
l   Overall coordination and timing of the turn

The tumble turn with the head leading

Order of limb movement during the turn

When the leading arm is about to pull after a fast swim in, the other arm joins it and they both pull together under the body. The head is simultaneously forced down and the body tucks tight for the somersault. The feet contact the wall after the somersault with the body still tucked. The legs extend vigorously and at the same time the shoulders twist to bring the body on to the breast. As the speed of the push falls away, the leg beat is picked up and one arm pull brings the body to the surface for a fast full stroke swim-out.

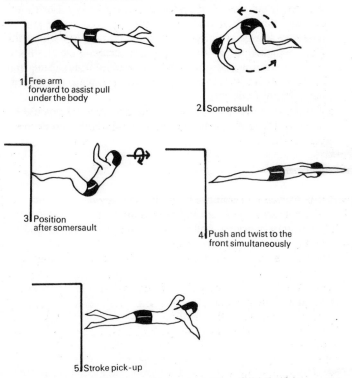

1 Free arm forward to assist pull under the body

2 Somersault

3 Position after somersault

4 Push and twist to the front simultaneously

5 Stroke pick-up

16   Tumble turn head leading

Demonstrations

Divide the demonstrations for this turn in to two parts. The fast swim-in and somersault bringing the feet to the wall are best seen from in front and above the swimmer. The push off and twist, leg and arm pick-ups and full stroke swim-out are visible from behind and above.

Practices

a   Demonstrate the turn in the water
b   Standing in shallow water get the pupil to push from the side with one arm leading. The free arm then joins the leading arm and both pull so the body somersaults to a standing position (best seen from behind and above)
c   Repeat exercise b after free swimming
d   Swim in slowly and repeat b up to the position where the feet are tucked to the wall. Repeat this exercise
e   From a starting position, grasp the rail and tuck. Sink and push off with a shoulder twist as the legs extend. Repeat this exercise until this is correct
f   Combine the skills to complete the turn. Practise this slowly at first but build up the pupil's speed as he becomes more proficient.

Points to watch for with learners

Check on the same points as for the tumble turn with the arm leading and also make sure that the free arm is joining the leading arm for a double arm pull under the body.

6

Water games and tricks

The water games and tricks I have described in this chapter are included for use in recreational periods to add balance and variety to lessons and to assist the pupil in gaining confidence in the water

The washing tub: sit in the water with the feet either tucked to the bottom or crossed at the ankles. Using only the hand-scull travel in different directions and spin around.

Washing tub racing: racing can be over given distances, round objects such as pupils standing in shallow water, or making a specific number of turns in one or two alternate directions.

Hand-sculling variations: get the pupil to lie prone or supine in the water with his arms sideways. Scull with the hands to move forwards head-first and then feet-first. Also try moving from a supine float position with the arms to the sides, first head-first, then feet-first and finally with the arms extended beyond the head. When sculling use the hands either with the palms facing backwards or opening and closing towards each other at shoulder width.

The doggy scull: this is an adaptation of the prone float. The hands are moved under the chest to propel the body forward and the head is kept clear of the water.

The rolling log: can be done from a prone or supine float position. The arms are held to the sides and the body kept straight. The swimmer then rolls over and over sideways using a hand-scull only. Use the hips and shoulders to assist the hands at first and just the hands when the movement is being done properly.

The sitting scull: sit as if in a chair and propel the body in various directions using the arms only. A variation to this game is to sit on a float and scull.

Walking the circle: get in a supine float position with one hand near the hip and the other at the back of the neck. The legs should be wide apart. Start walking around using the head as a pivot. All the limbs should be under water and do not turn the body on to the side. Take very large strides pressing the water with the soles of the feet.

Walking the waters: get in a vertical position in the water and do a breaststroke arm action with an exaggerated walking action. Point the toes and press the water with the backs of the legs and the soles of the feet, using steady gentle movements.

The lazy walk: get into a supine float position with the arms held to the sides. The lower legs should bend from the knees and do a walking action. Press the water with the backs of the legs and the soles of the feet. The body should progress feet first with steady gentle movements.

Double kick with scull: starting from a supine float position with the arms sideways and the lower legs bent from the knees. Kick both legs together with the feet touching and the thighs kept still. Assist this movement with a hand scull to achieve a head-first progress. For a feet-first progress bring the legs to the surface to commence the kick. Press the water with the backs of the legs and soles of the feet. It is essential to bring the legs to the surface for the next kick very gently, or progress will stop.

The turntable: commencing with a vertical float position slowly fold the arms and rest on the surface. Then spin the body using only leg movements and keeping the body straight.

The rolling float: starting in the back float position, sit up and grasp the ankles. Take a deep breath and hang on. The body will roll either forwards or backwards and then settle in a float. It is important to take a deep breath, to keep all movements gentle and deliberate and to grip the ankles firmly.

The Loch Ness float: get into a prone float position with the arms extended beyond the head. When the body is completely still, turn the palms upwards. Raise the head, then the bottom and finally lift the lower legs above the surface. All movements must be done gently to achieve the correct balance.

Many more floats and tricks can be made up using the above suggestions and combining them or building upon them in different ways.

Comedy strokes

Comedy strokes are merely a matter of using one's ingenuity and considerable fun can be had by experimenting within the safety limits. I will describe only a few of the more popular combinations.

The flutterbye stroke: start from the prone float position with the arms sideways. The arm action is a forward circular movement from the elbows only and making full use of the wrists. Bring the knees under the chest and kick straight back with the soles of the feet. The head can be in or out of the water, whichever is preferred by the individual pupil. The swimmer will not progress very far but the stroke is good fun.

The rising sun stroke: start from a prone float position and go into a loose tuck. The head should be under and the bottom above the surface of the water. Do a breaststroke arm action with the lower legs kicking alternately downwards.

The double periscope: get into a supine float position. Bring the lower legs above the surface keeping the trunk submerged. Propel the body forward with a sculling action.

The sneaky breaststroke: start in a prone float position and keep the body horizontal and straight throughout the stroke. If the swimmer is progressing to the right, the right leg and arm reach out and pull the water towards the body. The left leg and arm immediately push the water away from it. To progress to the left just reverse the procedure. Pointed toes help to propel the body with this stroke. As a variation it can be done in a supine position.

Possible stroke combinations

a   Breaststroke arms with front crawl legs
b   Front crawl arms with breaststroke legs
c   Side-stroke arms with front crawl legs
d   Butterfly legs with front crawl arms
e   Front crawl arms with butterfly legs
f   Backstroke arms with breaststroke legs
g   English backstroke arms with back crawl legs

Water games

It is important when playing water games that the teacher keeps *strict* discipline. Make sure that you, rather than the class, are in charge of the game as confusion in the water can be extremely dangerous.

Relay race: using the width of the pool get half of each team on one side of the bath and half on the other side. Each pupil dives in with the baton, which should be something light, and swims a width. He then climbs out and hands it over. Repeat this until one team wins by finishing.

Chinese Gala: use with the width of the pool for a relay race in which each swimmer performs a specified combination stroke as described in this chapter. The strokes can either be given to each swimmer before the race or they can be called out when each swimmer takes over.

The retrievers: for this game you need three or four teams. Place ping-pong balls or small floats in a rubber ring in the centre of the pool. The teams line up in opposite corners of the pool. The swimmer dives in, swims to the ring, retrieves one ball or float and swims on to the starting point before the next swimmer takes over. This can also be played with two or four individuals. The object is to retrieve all the objects one at a time, the winner being either the first team to get a stated number of objects or the one with the most objects in a given time.

The swap shop: two rubber rings are placed approximately seven to eight yards apart. The small objects described above are placed in one ring. The swimmer dives in, swims to the first ring, takes the objects out one at a time and places them in the other ring. This can be played by individuals or by teams which each have their own two rings. It is difficult to keep the rings in a static position unless they are held by other pupils. This adds to the fun and penalties can be awarded if the rings are brought closer together than a stated distance.

Push-of-war: two pupils get in a prone float position with one float between them and their arms extended. They then do the leg kick named by the teacher and try to push each other to the side of the bath or some other point. To utilize this game for team-work, use a bamboo pole and get the teams spaced alternately along the pole.

Wheel relay: it is important to remember that children get very excited in this game. You *must* insist on rules, such as no moving before they should, being kept. Keep the circles and line intact and play the game in water up to chest level only. Do *not* take your pupils into deep water until they are capable of treading water for long periods.

The first team stands shoulder-to-shoulder in a circle facing outwards. The second team stands in a line at arm's-length from one another and seven to eight yards from the circle, with one member three yards in front of the centre of the line. Number the teams off. The circle team proceeds with the first swimmer going round the circle and back to his place, then the second follows him and so on until the circle is complete as at the start. In the line the team member in front of the line swims to the highest numbered end of the line, and the second swims to take his place. The whole team moves down one place and the second swimmer moves to the end of the line. Repeat this until the line is complete as at the start of the game.

This game can be varied, for instance the team takes up positions as described above and the first swimmer in the circle team holds the ball or float. On the starting signal it is passed around the circle from hand to hand. Each time the first swimmer gets it he calls out to register that it has done a full circle. The pupil in the centre in front of the line team throws the ball to the second swimmer and he returns it to the first one, who then throws it to the third. The ball is returned each time to the first member. The first team has to make as many circles as possible before the second team has finished passing. Change the teams over to get the final result.

Fishing net: get the class standing in the water up to chest level. Two pupils join hands and the others can be anywhere they wish within the given depth. When they hear the signal, the two pupils who are holding hands begin the chase. Anyone whom they touch joins them and the game continues until all the pupils are in the chain with their hands joined.

Unfortunately it is impossible to enumerate all the games that can be played in this volume, but a little ingenuity and enthusiasm will keep your pupils happy for hours if necessary. An occasional game introduced into a swimming session will maintain their enthusiasm and interest.

7

Survival skills

Introduction

In this section of the book I will deal with specific survival skills, surface diving and the use of clothing. The death toll from drowning mounts steadily every year but few children and even fewer adults know how to help themselves in a drowning situation. I therefore feel that as many people as possible should acquire these skills in their own interests and this section of the book is intended to assist those who wish to do so. It is not my intention to teach survival techniques for the many tests that can be taken through the Amateur Swimming Association or the Swimming Teachers Association, as such manuals are already available. I merely wish to describe each skill and offer suggestions for teaching it. These skills can be used in whatever combination you require, according to your specific needs and aims.

Survival skills should be learnt as soon as possible, but the swimmer requires some basic skills before attempting them. He should be able to swim 800 metres, perform a variety of strokes proficiently and be able to tread water and float. If he can do all these things then it is safe to proceed with survival work.

Survival skills and how to build them up

Swimming: build up stamina with
a   Distance swimming, increasing the distances from one hundred to two hundred metres and up to a mile if required
b   Timed swims increasing progressively from a few minutes to half an hour or more
c   A combination of a and b so that the swimmer must cover a certain distance in a given time
d   Swimming set distances in clothes. Increase speed by trying to reduce personal best times over set but increasing distances

Build up an efficient variety of strokes for speed, resting and endurance.

Treading water: give timed exercises, lasting from one to five minutes or longer if required, in costumes and light garments, and then progress to outdoor clothes. Build up efficiency as described in the section on treading water.

Floating: practise all the floating methods in costumes and clothed. Then lengthen the time the floats last and vary the floating position. Change between floating, treading water and swimming and practise this with and without clothes.

Removal of clothing: teach how to remove clothing, building up confidence and efficiency with various types of clothes. Experiment to make sure which types of clothing are safe and which unsafe. All early removal work and float-making *must be done in shallow water.*

Making floats: experiment with various types of clothing for making floats to find the best material and the most suitable garments for float-making, together with the most efficient methods of inflation.

Surface diving practices

a   Head first
b   Feet first with and without clothes
c   From a swimming position
d   After treading water
e   Diving through hoops, partners' legs and so on wearing costumes
f   Diving to retrieve objects from the bottom
g   Changing direction under water to get objects spaced out on the bottom
h   Vary the distances for under water swimming up to a width, although adults can swim further if necessary

Re-surfacing methods

a   Fast return from the bottom with a leg push and the arms beyond the head
b   Fast return to the surface with leg kicks and full arm pulls
c   Slanting returns to avoid objects which are in the way
d   Swimming returns round or under objects

Entering the water: practise various types of entry from different heights. Combine this practice with re-surfacing and swimming away techniques with and without clothes.

Leaving the water: practise as many different ways of leaving the water as possible. Simulate the various likely conditions, such as slippery or steep banks, sharp rocks, poor handholds, or having to leave the water injured with a broken arm or with cramp. Also simulate assisting an injured partner to leave the water alone or with help.

Resuscitation: practise resuscitation as described in the section on life-saving, including the various methods of caring for the patient while waiting for assistance. Question the pupil on aspects of life-saving after he has been taken from the water, such as how to cover the drowning person, what you should give or not give him and how to recognise shock symptoms.

No time spent on survival skills is wasted. Give your pupil exercises which will build up an individual skill until it is efficient. Follow this up with others which will combine several or all of the skills. For example if the pupil is an efficient swimmer, a stamina swim could include surface diving, head and feet-first diving through a hoop, diving under a rope or to recover an object and a few yards' underwater swim. Many combinations of these skills can be used successfully. First set your target and then steadily work towards it.

How to remove clothing

The skill of removing clothing requires careful control to prevent panic when a garment sticks. It is *very important* that all early training in the techniques of removal is done in shallow water from waist to chest level and under strict supervision. Only when these techniques are mastered should a pupil be taken into deep water, but still only under strict supervision. In the early stages experiment with all types of garments and material to teach your pupil to distinguish which articles are safe and which unsafe. In teaching these skills the number of pupils is very important and you should teach only a single pupil if possible. If several pupils must be under instruction at the same time, class discipline should be strict and there should be assistance on hand if at all possible to look for potential danger. This is even more important in deep water.

Demonstrations and practices for beginners

Demonstrate the methods of removing clothes with verbal comments on the main points of safety and technique. After the demonstration the pupil should be allowed to attempt the whole skill *on land* and then parts of the skill in shallow water. Demonstrations of clothing removal are best given separately for the upper and the lower garments. If shoes are worn the pupil should first remove them and then proceed to take off the upper and lower garments

Removal methods

a   Demonstrate on land and then in the water, first in the shallow end and then in the deep end

b   Remove the short upper garment standing with the water up to shoulder level. First loosen the buttons or fasteners and ensure that there is a sufficent neck opening. Work the garment to the shoulder level and make sure the hands are grasping the top and bottom of the garment at the back of the neck. Finally remove it quickly over the head, either with the head above the water or else completely submerged

c   To remove the long upper garments practise this exercise standing in shallow water at shoulder level. Loosen the buttons or fasteners. Take the garment off the arms first, then take it down the body and remove it over the feet. Attempt this exercise first with the head above water, and then submerged

d   When these movements are correct, practise b and c again at a depth of about one foot above the pupil's height, but within reach of the teacher. When the pupil becomes confident and proficient take him into deeper water

e   Practices for removing the lower garments such as trousers and skirts should also initially take place in shallow water with the swimmer standing submerged to shoulder level. Loosen any buttons or fasteners, work the garment down to the ankles and remove it over the feet. Also practise submerging and removing the garment under water.

f   Repeat exercise e with the pupil about one foot out of his depth, but within the teacher's reach. Gradually go into deeper water as he gains confidence

g   Removal of the complete outfit can be attempted when the swimmer is proficient at the detailed practices for removing the upper and lower garments. Remove the complete outfit at a depth of a foot more than the pupil's height, but within the teacher's reach. Go into deeper water as the pupil's confidence and ability grows. Experiment by practising removing all the clothes, with different types of clothing.

Points to watch for with beginners

a   Correct techniques of removal
b   Quiet, deliberate and unhurried movements
c   Keep as much of the body as possible submerged
d   Do *not* tangle the clothing as it may be needed to make floats
e   Keep the pupil within reach of the side of the bath in deeper water
f   The pupil must be confident in shallow water *before* progressing to the deep end
g   If a garment sticks over his head *do not* allow the pupil to struggle but bring him in to the side and run through the technique again emphasising that he must make deliberate movements

Removal of footwear

Although the removal of footwear is not normally taught to children in swimming pools, the techniques should be practised and understood. For example, it would be pointless if a swimmer was expert at removing his trousers, if in an emergency he could not remove the shoes which prevent the trousers coming off. It is advisable to practise footwear removal using boots, shoes and wellingtons. Removal techniques should be demonstrated on land and in shallow and deep water, and the learner should face the teacher.

Summary of techniques

Raise the leg either at an angle across the other knee or in a partial tuck position to the chest. In both positions take a deep breath and then submerge to feel for the laces. If they are tied in a bow, feel for the ends and draw them gently apart. If they are in a knot then work it loose. When the laces have been loosened put the fingers in the sides of the shoes and pull sideways to loosen them. Then remove them by either:

a   Gripping the heel with one hand and removing them with a quick downwards and forwards movement
b   Gripping the heel with one hand, the toe of the shoe with the other and removing it with a forwards and downwards movement
c   Putting one foot at a right angle behind the other and removing the shoe with a downward pressure from the instep of the rear foot

Wellington boots are a problem because of the length of the boot and the suction that this causes. Work the boot down the leg with the hands and, once the ankle is clear of the foot portion, use method b or c as described above to remove it.

The pupil must have mastered these techniques in shallow water before going into deep water. He should also be able to submerge several times in succession to complete a practice.

Practices

a   Demonstrate the techniques on land and in the water
b   Practise the leg raising on land as described in a and b, above. Take a deep breath, lower the head with closed eyes and feel for the laces. Try this first with the bow and then with a tight knot. Loosen the footwear sideways with the fingers.
c   Practise the techniques described in the previous section on land with the boots or shoes untied. Stand to try out removal methods a and b, but sit for c
d   Practise removing wellington boots. Standing on land take a deep breath and lower the head with the eyes closed. Work the boot over the foot until the ankles are clear. Finally remove it by means of the methods described in the previous section

e   Standing in shallow water, repeat exercise b with sub-
    mergence. First try this with shoes and then with boots
    using methods a or b as described above for removal
f   Repeat e wearing wellington boots. Do not discard them
    once you have taken them off, but empty the water out, turn
    them upside down to trap the air and place them under the
    arms to use as floats
g   Repeat e at a depth one foot greater than the pupil's height.
    When he is proficient get him into deeper water
h   Repeat f at a depth of one foot more than the pupil's height,
    moving on to deeper water when he can do it correctly

Points to watch for with beginners

a   As much of the body should be submerged as possible
b   No tugging at the shoe laces
c   Quiet deliberate movements throughout
d   Make sure the footwear is loose enough to slip off quickly
e   Rest between the efforts to remove the shoes
f   Do not try to remove them too quickly as this upsets the
    balance and makes the shoes stick, which wastes the
    swimmer's energy
g   Wellingtons should be removed gently to prevent suction
    and sticking
h   Ensure good control and steady breathing
i   The eyes should be open but work by touch to be prepared
    for all possible conditions

The use of clothing as floats

There are three important points that the pupil should know
before he undertakes deep-water work using clothing as floats:
a   The types of clothing and material that make good floats
b   How to remove clothes without tangling them
c   How to use the float he has made to the best advantage
A rough guide to which kinds of material are suitable for
making floats is that most closely woven man-made fibres are
adequate and so are cotton, linen and light plastics. Do not be
afraid of experimenting in float-making. Tie off various com-

binations of openings to find the quickest effective way to collect air into the bag you have made.

In using floats, the guiding principle is to allow the float to ride high in the water to prevent the water pressure from forcing the air out again. Hang from the float rather than climbing on top of it. Experiment with various methods of using the float bearing this principle in mind. The ways in which the floats can be used will depend mostly on the size and shape of the bag which has been made. Remember that other items besides clothing often make excellent floats. Try using buckets, plastic or canvas bags, large cans or drums. If an object is light enough to handle and has a cavity in which you can trap air and seal it by submergence, it may make a good emergency float.

Inflating clothing to make a float

There are several established ways of inflating clothing which will be described here, but these are not the only methods which can be used. Do not be afraid to experiment with others as they may be equally effective. The object of the exercise is to inflate the clothing quickly and effectively, so any method which will achieve this aim should be used. Three important points should be remembered in relation to inflation:

a   Do not tangle the clothes when removing them
b   ʼBefore discarding anything think whether it could be useful
c   Do not waste valuable time and energy in inflating the wrong article. For example, you cannot inflate a string vest however much you try

Methods of inflation

Demonstrations of these methods of inflation should be given before starting any water practices. Always progress from land to shallow water and finally to deep water.

a   Tie off all openings except the smallest one and blow directly into it
b   Tie off all openings and blow through the wet material
c   Repeat method b by submerging and blowing through the wet material
d   Tie off all small openings and leave the largest. Hold the garment overhead in both hands. Bring it quickly forwards

and downwards through the surface of the water to trap the air, then immediately close the opening under water

e   Tie off all openings except one and hold this one just below the surface with one hand. Cup the other hand and plunge it through the surface to the opening. Repeat this movement rapidly to inflate the article and when it is inflated close the opening under water.

The type of inflation method which is used will depend entirely on the garment to be inflated. A kit bag or pillow case could be inflated by method e but this would waste valuable time, so method d would be more effective. Method d would not be effective to inflate a cotton vest, but any of the other methods would work.

In practice, inflation is a matter of experiment and common-sense. In a situation where survival is at stake, the swimmer can only think if he is calmly in control. To achieve this he must utilise all the survival skills which he possesses and his ability to do this is a matter of good basic training.

Surface diving and underwater swimming

Surface diving and underwater swimming are often neglected, but they form an essential part of survival work. They are also used in many recreational activities and are worth learning both for pleasure and to achieve increased safety in the water. There are two recognised ways of diving beneath the surface, either head-first or feet-first, and both have their specific uses according to particular circumstances. If a swimmer moving forwards wishes to submerge quickly, it is easier to use the head-first method as it forms a continuation of his forward progress. On the other hand if he is treading water and wishes to pass under an object immediately in front of him, it is easier to use the feet-first method.

The head-first surface dive

Order of limb movements

Lie in the prone position on the surface. The head is pushed forwards and downwards, at the same time as the body is bent at the waist and the arms pull under the body to the thighs. The legs are held together, raised in line with the trunk and allowed to slip through the surface of the water. The body is *not* kicked under the surface by the legs.

Demonstration and practices

The trunk bend and the arm pull should be demonstrated on land and in the water, and can be seen from the swimmer's front and side. The leg movement should be shown with the swimmer at a shoulder level depth. He stands with his arms above his head and springs from the bottom into a handstand. The legs are kept straight together as they lift to come in line with the trunk. The pupil should see this movement from the side of and from behind the swimmer.

a Demonstrate the movements as described above
b Stand up in shallow water up to chest level, bend from the waist and then stand up again
c Repeat exercise b, adding arm pull as you bend from the waist
d Standing in shallower water up to waist level, bend and put the hands on the bottom of the pool. Raise the legs together and, keeping them straight, try to get into a handstand position
e Lying in the prone position in shallow water push from the side and do a full movement to a handstand
f Repeat e at a depth one foot above the pupil's height. When he becomes more adept at this move into deeper water
g Repeat f from a moving position such as swimming forward. Surface and repeat the exercise
h Starting as for exercise f, repeat e doing the armstroke again when submerged. Adopt an under water swimming position which is horizontal with the head lower than the feet. Complete two full breaststroke cycles and then surface. Repeat this exercise until it is correct
i Combine all these techniques in deep water after a forwards movement. Swim four to five yards under water before surfacing. Repeat this as many times as seems necessary

The methods described above are for when you are swimming breaststroke or butterfly. To do the head-first surface dive from the front crawl the body is piked downwards as described above. As the pulling arm enters, the other arm comes forward to assist, and the rest of the movement is as for the breaststroke.

The head-first surface dive from the backstroke

The head-first surface dive from the backstroke is rarely taught to beginners, since it requires greater coordination than they can usually master. As the leading arm pulls, the body is flipped over into the prone position at the same time as the bend at the waist. The turn is made on the same side as the pulling arm. The rest of the movement is as previously described. Most backstroke swimmers prefer to throw the head well back as the leading arm pulls, simultaneously arching the back when the legs lift. In effect they perform a half-somersault with the body almost straight just prior to the flip-over for submergence.

Points to watch for with beginners

a   Timing of the movement, especially the simultaneous pike and pull
b   Legs together and straight
c   No kicking with the legs on submergence
d   The legs should move up fast
e   Shallow pull
f   Not forcing the head under
g   Sticking the chest out
h   Not pulling to the thighs when submerging

Surface diving feet-first

Sequence of the stroke

Starting from a treading water position, the legs give a vigorous scissors or breaststroke kick as the palms of the hands press downwards. The body rises from the water and the swimmer breathes, then the arms are placed at the sides. Now that the body is straight it sinks rapidly and the swimmer can assist the descent by sweeping his arms sideways and upwards. Learners are often taught to sink with their arms overhead but this tends to have a braking effect if they try to use the arms to assist their descent.

Demonstrations and practices

The pupil must be able to tread water before attempting these exercises.

a   Demonstrate the feet first surface dive

b   Get the pupil to tread water at a depth two or three feet above his height. Slowly reduce the movement to a minimum, keeping the arms sideways between the shoulders and the waist

c   Repeat exercise b, adding a kicking movement and sweeping the arms downwards. Repeat this until it is correct and the movements are properly timed, then take him into deeper water

d   Repeat c in deep water. When the body is submerged, tuck it forward into a swimming position. Do a two-stroke cycle and then surface

e   Combine the above skills and swim four or five yards under water

f   Vary these exercises. Combine the head-and feet-first dives with short swims under water or across the width of the pool

Points to watch for with beginners

a   Strong vigorous kick

b   Good height out of the water after kicking

c   Body straight after the kick

d   Arms to the sides to assist the descent

e   Palms facing outwards ready for the upward sweep

f   Deep breathe before submerging

Swimming under water

Swimming under water is a useful ability as it forms the basis for many water games and also for diving, as well as having survival value. After submerging the body tends to surface automatically. To offset this, the head is kept slightly below the level of the feet when swimming horizontally under water. The arm pull plays an important part in maintaining this position and it should be in a backwards and slightly upwards direction. To conserve the swimmer's energy his strokes should be strong, slow and rhythmic. A suggested under water stroke is the doggy paddle arm action, which involves reaching forward with alternate arms and pulling straight under the body, combined with a normal front crawl leg action. The breaststroke is always useful, either as normal stroke with an arm pull through to the thighs, or with a front crawl leg movement. These are the more popular underwater strokes, but you can experiment with other combinations according to the pupil's ability. No practice suggestions have been included in this section because once the pupil has mastered the surface swimming strokes he will automatically adapt them as under water strokes. The suggested combinations are only intended as a guide to the teacher.

Getting into the water

Although getting into the water may appear very simple, it is not always as easy as it seems and under certain circumstances it can be quite a problem. For example in strange surroundings such as a dock, a promenade or a lake with high banks where for some urgent reason the swimmer may be forced to enter the water, he may experience considerable difficulty. In addition the water below may be deep or shallow, clear or filthy, strewn with surface debris or concealing hidden obstacles beneath the surface. The swimmer does not know but he may still have to go in. The important thing under these circumstances is *never to dive in*, but always to jump. Even the way the swimmer jumps will depend on several factors and these are some ways of jumping in safely:

a Jump in from both feet rather than one because this lessens the likelihood of the body rotating in the air
b Step off into the water. *Never* run and jump in because you may spin and stepping in gives more control in the air
c If you must look down into the water only use the eyes and never tilt the head forwards when jumping, as you may suffer a neck or facial injury

Entering the water and preventing the body from going too deep

a Jump outwards keeping the body under control as the water has a braking effect on forward momentum b   On entering spread the limbs quickly because this provides a greater braking effect

c   Tuck the body to strike the surface and spread the limbs *immediately* the surface has been broken

It is important that the limbs are spread after striking the surface, so as to avoid groin or shoulder injuries. The legs can either be split sideways or to the front and rear.

Deep entries

a   Step off on one foot only and keep the body erect. The head should be up and the arms to the sides

b   Jump from both feet together keeping the body erect, the head up and the arms to the sides

Points to watch for with beginners

a   Control the step or jump-off. The body should be erect and the head up without strain

b   Arms hanging relaxed at the sides

c   No rotation either forwards or backwards

d   Do not tilt the head to look down

e   The limbs should spread after striking the surface

f   If running to take off do not lean forward on the take-off

Survival strokes after entry

Having entered the water and re-surfaced, the immediate problem is to swim to safety or last out until help arrives. The actual course of action will depend on the circumstances, so it is wise to practise different kinds of swimming using the stroke best suited to the particular situations envisaged. If a deep entry has been made into water which has debris falling into it, an inclined swim away from the area is indicated to avoid injury. Good strokes to use under these circumstances would be the underwater breaststroke or the breaststroke arms and front crawl legs. Once he is safely on the surface the swimmer needs the fastest possible stroke to get him clear of the danger area. If a shallow entry has been made, there is no danger from the surface and help is in sight, no under water stroke is needed. The swimmer may then require a resting stroke on the surface, such as normal or inverted breaststroke, side-stroke, life-saving backstroke, treading water or a float position.

If the swimmer has re-surfaced with no help in sight and a long swim ahead, speed is pointless. Physical strength and mental stability should be preserved and under these conditions the whole range of survival skills may have to come into play. The swimmer may have to remove his clothes, make and inflate floats, float, tread water and then use all the resting strokes in turn if he is to survive.

Getting out of the water

If the swimmer has survived an emergency and reached an exit point, he then has to climb out. This is often the greatest problem of all and many people have drowned because of it, so do not ignore this vital aspect of survival. Although apparatus for simulating natural conditions is not available in the average swimming pool, there are still many ways in which a little ingenuity can enable the teacher to cover the various methods of getting out of the water. I have included some suggestions which can be built upon to increase the degree of difficulty involved in the exercise.

Use of steps

a   Exit without using the handrails, first wearing a costume and then fully clothed
b   Simulate a limb injury and then exit from the pool with and without using the rails
c   Assist an exhausted partner to get out of the water with and without the rails
d   Assist an injured partner to leave the water wearing clothes
e   Assist each other out of the water when both partners are injured in different limbs

Use of the side of the bath

a   Get out of deep water unassisted after a long swim, then repeat this fully clothed

b   Assist an exhausted partner in shallow and then in deep water
c   Simulate injuries in one and then both of the partners, and practise getting out of first shallow and then deep water
d   Exit over a slippery surface such as a smooth rubber mat
e   Leave the water over a slippery surface individually, then with partners and finally simulating injuries
f   Secure an injured partner at the side and then go for help
g   Place an obstacle at the exit point and get out over it, first wearing a bathing costume and then fully clothed.

Use of poles, ropes and planks

a   Exit up first a vertical rope and then an inclined one. Practise this fully clothed
b   Assist the partner up an inclined rope at the side, first in shallow and then in deep water
c   Exit via an inclined pole or plank
d   Suspend a rope over the side lengthways and progress along the rope to the exit point
e   Suspend a rope as for exercise d, secure the injured partner to the rope and then go to the exit point for help

There are a great many possible situations and exercises that can be practised with these props, although normally poles ropes and planks are not allowed. Other equipment found in most swimming pools, such as diving bricks, hoops, bamboo poles, floats and rings, can be used in simulation exercises to give your pupil the practice in coping with an unexpected situation and to test his watermanship and stamina.

Only after personally seeing the results of drowning can one really appreciate the value of survival work. A little knowledge of survival skills would often have been the deciding factor between life and death. Parents and teachers should ensure that children master the basic survival skills so that they can safely enter the water.

8
Life-saving techniques

This section describes some of the skills used in swimming rescue but it forms only a part of the wider subject of life-saving and is not intended as a study of all its aspects. To attempt a rescue without the proper training, a knowledge of different methods and a wide background of safety knowledge is to place your own life in danger. The reader is strongly recommended to study the handbook of the Royal Life Saving Society and join a class for full instruction in life-saving skills.

Approaching a drowning person

Always approach a drowning person with extreme caution. If he succeeds in grasping the rescuer both lives may be lost. It is essential to approach cautiously, develop the ability to stop forward motion instantly and rapidly back away from the drowning person. Practise this by getting into a prone float position. Throw the head and shoulders quickly backwards, at the same time driving the water towards the feet with a vigorous sculling action.

If the drowning person is close enough to clutch you as you back away, use your hands, feet or shoulders against his chest to push him away quickly.

17   Practice retreat

18   Foot on chest push-off

If he grasps your leg despite your efforts, *don't hesitate* to tread him under water. As soon as his head is submerged and approximately level with your chest, grasp his chin and turn him quickly into a towing position. If he is very close and attempts to clutch you, place your head under his chin and grasp his waist, chest or arms. Either push him upwards immediately or submerge and then do so.

Releases

If you are grasped despite your efforts it is *imperative* that you release yourself as quickly as possible or you may both be lost. You must be absolutely ruthless in releasing yourself at this stage. The methods of release described here have been proved effective but any method will suffice if it achieves the immediate objective of freeing the rescuer.

If you are clutched round the neck drop your head quickly and rest your chin on your chest. Exert pressure on the person's elbows or arms and push him up and away. Your knee in his groin will be very effective in making him release you.

If you are clutched round the upper arms and trunk force

19 · Treading under when the leg is grasped

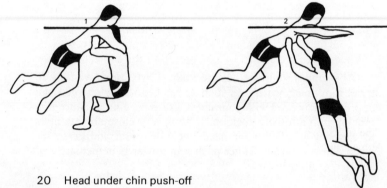

20 Head under chin push-off

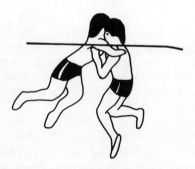

21 Clutched round the neck

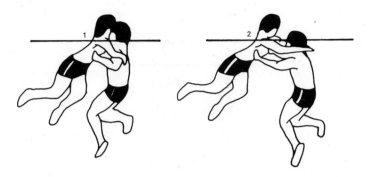

22   Clutched round the upper arms and trunk

your elbows outwards and place your palms under the person's armpits or on his trunk. Inhale deeply, submerge, slip downwards out of his clutch and turn him quickly ready for towing.

When you are clutched by one arm with the subject holding you with both hands, there are two possible ways of extricating yourself. Pull the person towards you by the trapped arm and put the free arm round the back of his neck to grasp his chin. Kick vigorously in the water to raise yourself up behind him. The trapped arm may come free, but even if it is still trapped the subject will be in a good towing position.

The second method of freeing your arm is to clench the fist of the trapped arm, reach either over or under with the free arm, depending on how it is trapped, and between his arms. Grasp your own clenched fist and pull it either upwards or downwards, at the same time applying pressure to his thumb joints. This should break you apart. Establish contact again immediately and turn the person to a towing position.

If you are clutched from the rear either round the neck or the trunk, grasp one wrist with the opposite hand and place the

23   Clutched by one arm (1)

24   Clutched by one arm (2)

other one under the person's elbow. Pull downwards and inwards on his wrist. Force his elbow up, simultaneously turning your head away from his elbow so you can slip out under his arm. Maintain your hold on his wrist until you have turned it behind his back and he is in a towing position. If you are grasped in this way round the neck, protect your throat by immediately forcing your chin down to your chest.

An alternative method of releasing yourself from a grip from the rear is to grasp the person's thumbs or fingers and bend them quickly back against the joints. This is painful and will usually successfully free you.

If you are confronted by two swimmers in difficulties who are locked together your first efforts should be directed towards the weaker one, or the one in greater danger. Approach the chosen person from behind and grasp his chin with both hands. Bear down on him with the forearms and submerge *both* swimmers. Bring one foot over the chosen person's locked arms and place it on the other person's chest. Push them apart by a vigorous leg extension, at the same time pulling the one you are rescuing upwards and backwards ready for towing.

Summary

These are the recognised methods of releasing yourself, but it is safer to avoid being clutched in the first place, so always approach a drowning person cautiously and develop the ability

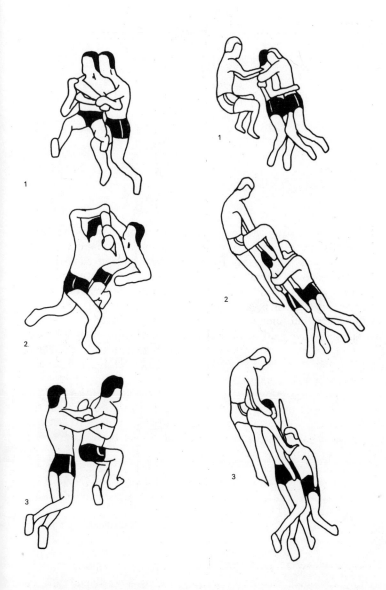

25 Clutched from the rear   26 Two swimmers locked together

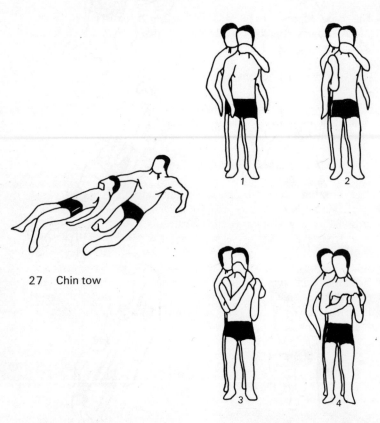

27   Chin tow

28   Controlling the subject

to stop immediately and back away. If you are clutched, you *must* release yourself as quickly as possible and be absolutely ruthless doing this.

Towing

The type of tow to be used will depend on the particular circumstances, and so it is advisable to practise all the methods which are described here.

Hair, chin or loose clothing tow

If the person is quiet and cooperative, you can grasp his hair, chin or loose clothing and tow him with your arm extended, using side-stroke or life-saving backstroke.

Chin tow for a person needing control

Pass your arm over his shoulder and cup his chin in your hand. Tuck his head into your shoulder and use your free arm to assist you in swimming on your back. If he struggles, pass your free arm under his armpit and take a firm grip on his shoulder from the front. If he still struggles, clamp the hand holding his chin over his mouth and pinch his nose between the finger and thumb to stop him breathing temporarily. The normal reaction to this is that the subject will pull your arm down to his chest and hold it there. Continue towing him in this position.

Towing in choppy conditions

Place one arm over the person's shoulder and across his chest and grasp him under the armpit. Use your free hand to do a semi-side-stroke. If he struggles, place your free hand under his armpit and pull his shoulder firmly to your chest. When using your free arm to swim,

29   Towing in choppy conditions

keep your hip in the small of the person's back to keep him horizontal.

Towing two people

Provided the two people are quiet and cooperative they can both be towed at the same time by grasping them by the hair, the chin or the clothing at the back of their necks. Use a leg kick such as inverted breaststroke or the life-saving kick to swim along.

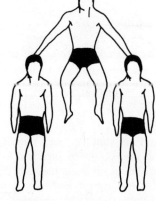

30   Towing two subjects

Summary on releases and tows

Although I have only described standard methods of releasing and towing, these are only intended as a guide. The rescuer must use intelligence and ingenuity to cope with the particular circumstances. The drowning person will be equally grateful whatever methods you have rescued him by, as the object of the exercise is to save him, not to dazzle him with your command of the techniques.

Landing a rescued person

After rescuing someone, the final step to safety is often very difficult. He may be injured, unconscious or even unco-operative and it is wise to practise various techniques for getting him on dry land.

Landing an injured or unconscious person

You may have to support the person before you can actually land him. Turn his back towards you and slip your arms beneath his armpits. Grip the side of the pool, the bank or any other available support and ascertain that his face is clear of the water. Keep him suspended in this way until he is ready to land.

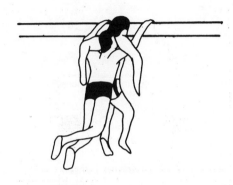

31   Support in the water

32   Landing on beach or shelving surface

Landing on a shelving beach or other slope

As soon as you can stand on the bottom, place your arms under his armpits and float him in by walking backwards.

Landing an uninjured co-operative person

Support an uninjured person against the side until he is ready to land. Reach under water

33   Landing uninjured and co-operative person

and cup one or both of your hands. Place his foot or lower leg in the cup and help him to get out of the water by lifting.

Landing an injured or unconscious person

Support an injured person as described until he is ready to land, then place his hands one on top of the other on the landing

34   Securing and climbing
     out

point. Put your own hand on top to secure him and your other hand on the side of the bath. Press down on your hands so you can leave the water yourself. He can then be lifted out either by the cross arm lift in which you cross your own hands and take the person's wrists. Raise and lower him two or three times to gain momentum and then give a final lift to the landing point, un-crossing your arms as you do so. This turns him on to his back. You can also use the

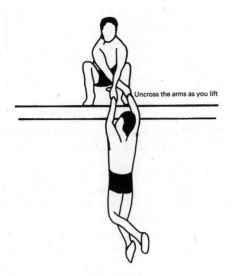

Uncross the arms as you lift

35   Cross-arm lift

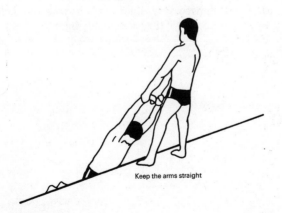

Keep the arms straight

36   Straight-arm lift

straight arm lift in which you take hold of the person's wrists without crossing your hands. Raise and lower him and finally lift him to bend his trunk over the side. Secure him with one hand and then reach down to raise his legs to the side.

37 Carrying a
rescued
person

Carrying the rescued person

You may be required to carry someone you have rescued up steps or a shelving bank. The easiest way to do this is to use the 'fireman's lift'. Stand the person up sufficiently to get your arm between his legs. Rest his trunk across your shoulders, leaving one of his arms hanging free. Put your arm between his legs and then forward over his leg to grasp the hanging arm by the wrist and draw it across your chest. This secures him and leaves your other arm free to assist your progress.

Although these are the accepted methods of landing people, they are only intended for guidance. Other methods may be equally effective according to the circumstances. You must be very careful to avoid unnecessary injury when you are helping someone to land, especially if they are already injured.

9

Resuscitation

The techniques of resuscitation are vital not only for water safety but also in many situations in everyday life where quick and decisive action could mean the difference between life and death. Although there are several methods of resuscitation, I will only deal with the expired air method because it can be easily learnt and quickly applied, as well as having been proved very effective since it was introduced.

Resuscitation positions

Learning expired air techniques

a   Practise breathing deeply in and out at five-second intervals
b   *Resuscitation via the nose:*
    Place the head in the correct position
    Close the mouth
    Support the jaw by placing your thumb and forefinger down either side of the jaw bone. Curl the rest of the fingers and fit the knuckle of the second finger under the jaw, making sure that your curled fingers do not press on the throat
c   *Resuscitation through the mouth:* the procedure is the same except that the mouth is open and kept that way by the hand holding the jaw. The nose is closed between the forefinger and thumb of the other hand
d   Practise the correct position for the operator by kneeling close to the practice partner
e   Where possible practise these techniques on a training manikin or mask
f   If no training aid is available for practice and demonstration purposes, lean over the partner and breathe down past his cheek
g   Practise turning the partner from the front to the back for resuscitation as follows:
    Kneel by his side
    Stretch out the arm nearest to you beyond his head

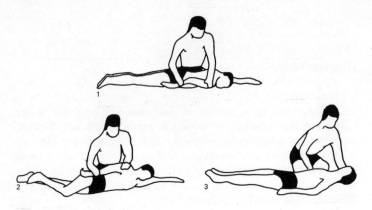

38   Resuscitation positions

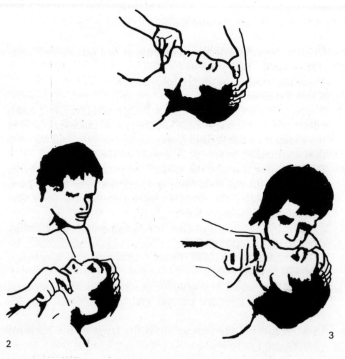

39   Expired air resuscitation method

Grasp the shoulder farthest away from you with one hand, then simultaneously grasp his hip and clamp his wrist with the other
Roll him over against your thigh
Lower him gently to the ground, supporting his head and shoulders as you do so
Replace the extended arm by his side

40   Vomiting

Procedure for expired air resuscitation

a   Never delay in giving assistance
b   *Keep calm*
c   Lay the person on his back if possible, with the head a little higher than the feet
d   Tilt the head back and lift the jaw. This should move the tongue away from the throat, which is a common cause of blockage. One of three things may now happen. Normal breathing may begin at once and consciousness quickly return. The patient's colouring should become pink but watch carefully in case breathing stops again. Normal breathing may commence, but consciousness may *not* return. In this case place the person on his front with his head turned to one side and the arm on this side bent to take the weight of the shoulder. One leg should be stretched behind and the other bent at the knee. Keep the airways clear and consciousness may then return. This is called the 'coma position'. Breathing may return, but may be noisy, showing that the airways are not fully clear. Try to clear them as there may be fluid in the throat
e   If breathing does not start again, clear the mouth and throat of any obvious obstruction such as fluid or vomit
f   If there is still no sign of breathing after clearing, proceed as follows:
Close the person's mouth and breathe gently but firmly into his nose, or pinch his nose between your finger and thumb and blow gently but firmly into his mouth. As you do this his chest will rise

Turn your head away. Inhale and watch for his chest to fall

Give him four quick breaths and then continue with one breath every five seconds, so that he is getting twelve breaths a minute

If the chest does not rise and fall either you are making a poor seal over the mouth or nose, or the airway is still blocked and needs clearing again

If the airway is clear, it will not be long before the pink skin tint replaces the blue one caused by suspended respiration

As consciousness returns the patient will start to breathe on his own. This is the time to stop resuscitation, but continue holding his chin up to keep the airways clear

If he vomits, turn him onto his side, away from you. Clear his mouth and throat with your finger, then return him to his back and start resuscitation again if necessary

If you are treating a baby, the procedure is as above except that you should make a seal over his nose and mouth with your mouth. Breathe very gently into his *mouth* with a puff of the cheeks and repeat this at a rate of twenty to twenty-five times per minute. *Never* blow hard into a baby's lungs.

Air in the stomach

If the airway is only partially cleared, air may enter the stomach. This causes swelling in the upper part of the stomach but gentle pressure will push this out quite safely. If this clearance should make the patient sick, turn him on to his side and clear the mouth and throat before starting resuscitation efforts again.

Techniques in water

Use the mouth to nose method in the water. Close the person's mouth and support the jaw as described for this technique.

Standing in shallow water: support the person's trunk either between his shoulder blades or under his farther armpit. Give resuscitation as described above with your free arm supporting his jaw.

Supporting in deep water: support the person by gripping the bar or holding onto something else, with your free hand cradling his head in the crook of your arm.

Swimming in deep water: support him with your free hand

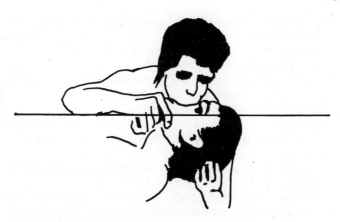

41   Resuscitation techniques in water

under the back of his head. Keep his face clear of the water but avoid twisting his head. Keep him moving slowly with his body in a normal towing position.

After resuscitation every casualty should immediately be taken to hospital, by ambulance if necessary, for a medical check-up.

Emergencies

Severe external bleeding may have to be stopped before resuscitation can begin. The quickest way is to apply pressure over the actual site of the bleeding. You can apply a pad and bandages later if necessary. However resuscitation must not be delayed unless bleeding is very severe.

Shock will always be present to some degree under these circumstances but it is accentuated by cold, loss of blood, pain and fear. When the patient is in shock he will appear pale, his skin will be cold and moist, his pulse weak and his breathing shallow. The best treatment for shock is:

a   Comfort and reassure the casualty
b   Be gentle
c   Remove him only if it is necessary
d   Lie him with his legs raised if possible
e   Loosen his clothing at the neck and waist
f   Stop any bleeding

g   Cover him to keep him warm under and over the body
h   Do *not* give food or drink
i   Do *not* warm him by artificial means
j   Send for medical help *immediately*

The effects of cold may lead to a general deterioration in condition. The treatment for cold should be as follows:

a   If he is dry, wrap him in warm covers to prevent him losing further heat
b   If he is wet and unclothed, dry him quickly and wrap him as described above
c   If he is wet and clothed, wrap him in dry blankets or clothing

Cramp is a constant painful contraction of a muscle. The best treatment is to stretch the limb and warm it by rubbing or, if it is in the back or the stomach, just warm it by rubbing the area.

  One cannot over-emphasise the importance of resuscitation skills, as knowledge of them may be literally a matter of life or death.

10

Anatomy and physiology

This chapter is not intended as a study of anatomy and physiology but rather as an outline of the functions of the body and muscles during swimming. It is useful for the teacher to know about the sources of energy and how it is transmitted to and used by muscular tissues during exercise. He will then understand why swimming takes such a rapid toll of the swimmer's energy during the initial teaching stages.

There are two basic sources of energy, food and air. Food is broken down and altered chemically by the body into blood sugars. These are absorbed into the blood stream and carried to the tissues. Oxygen is taken in through the lungs, absorbed into the blood stream and carried to the tissues. These two resources are necessary for the energy subsequently used up by exercise. As a result of exercise a residue of waste is left in the muscle tissues, and it is this waste which is the primary cause of fatigue. Since it is impossible to detail the organic processes involved in the removal of this waste in this volume, it will be sufficient if the reader understands that it is *vital* to remove this waste as quickly as possible if exercise is to continue.

The most important thing to remember is that each individual has a definite endurance limit for any unaccustomed physical activity. The first indication of this approaching limit is fatigue, which can range from mere lethargy as regards further effort to a profound physical or mental exhaustion.

During exercise the immediate requirement of the body is for more oxygen to replace that which is being burnt in the tissues. This is achieved automatically in several ways:

a   The heart pumps faster, considerably increasing the blood supply to the tissues
b   The rate and depth of breathing increases substantially
c   The blood pressure rises
d   Other systems such as the digestive system will have their blood supply decreased
e   The circulation is stimulated to dispose of tissue wastes more quickly

All these changes are set in motion by tiny nerve endings in the arteries, which are sensitive to the build-up of carbon dioxide. Teachers should take particular note of the withdrawal of blood supplies from other areas such as the digestive system. Because the reduced digestive processes during exercise may cause stomach cramp, children *must* be discouraged from eating just before or during swimming lessons.

Fatigue build-up

When you are learning any new physical skill the output of energy in relation to the efficiency of the movement is considerable. In a learner swimmer it is often colossal, for the following reasons:

a   Working in an unnatural element
b   Instinctive fear of this element
c   Partial loss of gravity through buoyancy causes inefficient muscle use
d   Disorientation caused by water splashing in the eyes and mouth
e   Faster and shallower breathing caused by fear or excitement
f   Lack of oxygen due to this inadequate breathing
g   Lack of oxygen causes rapid build-up of carbon dioxide in the tissues
h   Inefficient teaching may give inadequate rest to the pupil

The teacher should be aware that within a class of perhaps twenty children there will be great variations in individual fitness. The body is capable of withstanding non-renewal of its oxygen for a short period. The length of this period will however depend entirely on the fitness of the particular person. This period is known as the oxygen debt, and in effect exercise is maintained during this period by using the residue of oxygen in the body. A trained athlete can continue exercising for an appreciable time compared with an untrained person, but this is a strenuously acquired skill. This 'debt' is repaid when one takes a rest to allow the various body systems to return to normal and to dispose of waste products. If the swimmer does not rest, the carbon dioxide waste will gradually build up in the muscle tissues, at a rate depending on the severity of the activity and the fitness of the person.

The first danger sign is a feeling of tiredness, either physical or mental, or sometimes both. The second danger signal is cramp, which is a painful muscular contraction. If the person is made to continue exercising at the same rate, the waste build-up will rapidly become acute and unconsciousness will follow. There have been several recorded instances in sport when the waste build-up was so complete that death resulted. Fortunately, although fatigue and cramp are quite common, the fatal build-up rarely occurs. However, the dangers should not be ignored.

It is clear that the ability to fend off fatigue depends on how quickly the body can remove waste and replenish itself with fresh oxygen. On land this is reasonably easy because everyone automatically breathes more deeply in exercise, but in swimming two factors inhibit the pupil:

a   To breathe easily the mouth must be clear of the water
b   Even in shallow water water pressure on the rib-cage inhibits the expansion of the lungs and therefore makes deep breathing difficult.

Because of these factors oxygen supplies cannot be replaced easily in the learning stages of swimming. The teacher must always be aware of the physical state of the pupil, *especially in class work*, and this is why I have stated elsewhere in the book that adequate rest *must* be given at frequent intervals whatever the pupil's age.

I also consider it essential that all swimming teachers should retain their 'feel' of the water by some personal practice. They must know the difficulties of the exercises they give and be fully aware of the fatigue factors involved. This is important, especially when the instructor himself is inexperienced or if he is a friend, parent or well-intentioned bystander, as such people tend to ask their pupils to do the impossible. It is particularly important when dealing with handicapped pupils, because in addition to the normal problems they also bear the burden of their disabilities.

Fear plays a vital part in causing fatigue, as it creates tremendous muscular tension which rapidly burns valuable energy. It also renders muscle action inefficient, which in turn adds to the build-up of waste when the pupil is attempting the skill. To force a child to attempt any skill in water when he is obviously terrified is not just culpable stupidity—it is positively dangerous. It is also pointless telling the child to relax because he cannot consciously do so. It is only when the pupil's mind is relaxed that his body will be. The simplest way to achieve this is to divert his mind by making him happy, and this is why learning to swim or dive should be made a pleasure rather than a punishment.

Panic

People are often amazed that it is possible for a child or even an adult to drown in a crowded pool. The truth is that unless due care is taken this is frighteningly easy. There is a popular misconception that people who are in danger of drowning shout and thrash about, but this rarely happens. In an uncontrolled situation the potential victim first feels frightened. Increasing tension first grips the mind and then the body: the person's breathing becomes swift and shallow and his muscles tense so that they can only achieve ineffective movement. This produces waste at an alarming rate and a vicious circle of fear and energy loss is set in motion. Disorientation follows and the victim sinks into mental confusion as the water inhibits his sight, hearing and breathing. He gives way to irrational panic, becoming numb with shock, this is in its turn replaced by an unnatural quietness. The swimmer stiffens with silent terror and quietly but helplessly slips beneath the surface where he may lie unnoticed on the bottom, quietly drowning in the midst of all the other swimmers.

It is *imperative*, especially when school children are taught as a class during public swimming time, that the teacher should always have all his pupils in view. This is easier if they all wear coloured caps as these make them immediately identifiable.

The anatomy of swimming strokes

Firstly it must be remembered that muscles do not work singly and any given action is the result of the combined effort of a group of muscles. In fact many muscles have several sets of fibres and each set is designed to perform a different function. For example, the deltoid or shoulder muscle has three sets of fibres: anterior, medial and posterior. The first takes the arm forwards, the second lifts it and the third takes it backwards. To help the reader to understand about the muscles I will define some of the terms used in anatomy to describe movements.

Flexion is to take forward, ie to bend the arm towards the shoulder.

Extension is to take backwards and means to straighten the arm.

Abduction is to move away and thus involves moving the arm or leg sideways.

Adduction is to bring towards the body.

Rotation means to turn about on its own axis, ie. turning the head from side to side.

Circumduction is a circular movement, such as swinging the arm round at the shoulder joint.

Dorsal means relating to the upper back.

Lumbar means relating to the lower back.

Dorsiflexion is bending the foot and toes upwards.

Plantar is of the sole of the foot.

Plantar flexion is bending the foot downwards towards the ground.

Anterior means the front of the body.

Posterior is the back of the body.

The *midline* is an imaginary line running vertically down the centre of the body.

An efficient respiratory system is vital for swimming. These are the main muscles involved and their approximate locations and functions.

The *Diaphragm* forms the floor of the thorax or chest and the roof of the abdomen. Its function is respiration and expulsion.

The *rectus abdominus* is situated in front of the abdomen and it flexes the thorax when exhaling.

The *oblique externus abdominus* lies to the front and side of the abdomen.

The *oblique internus abdominus* lies beneath the *externus*.

The *transversalis abdominus* lies beneath the *internus*. These last three muscles work with the *rectus abdominus* and perform the same function in respiration.

The *quadratus lumborum* lies in the lumbar region of the back. It keeps the spine straight and assists in the contraction of the diaphragm.

The *serratus posticus superior* lies in the upper part of the back and raises the ribs during inhalation.

The *serratus posticus inferior* lies at the junction of the lumbar and dorsal regions of the back and fixes the ribs in respiration.

The *scalenus muscles* are in the neck. Anterior, medius and posterior muscles assist in fixing the ribs during respiration.

The *serratus magnus* lies between the ribs and the shoulder blade in the upper part and to the side of the chest. It not only assists in raising the ribs in respiration, but is the chief muscle used when one is pushing something.

Muscles used in the front crawl arm movement and breathing

The most difficult aspect of the front crawl is the breathing, as it can upset the balance of the body if it is done inefficiently. The muscle mainly concerned in this head movement is the sterno-mastoid which is situated obliquely on either side of the neck. The left side will bend the head to the left and the right side to the right but in this stroke the head should be *turned* rather than bent so that the muscle on the left will turn the face to the right and vica versa. If the head is lifted and turned to breathe this is done by the trapiezius, located at the back of the neck and covering the shoulders, and also the splenis, at the back of the neck and in the upper dorsal region of the back. The correct movement is to turn the head to avoid upsetting the balance of the body by bringing other muscles into play. When starting the front crawl pull, the hand enters the water and meets its resistance. The pectoralis major and minor covering the front of the upper chest and the armpit supply the necessary power. The coraco-brachialis, in the upper and inner side of the arm, helps the arm to go forwards and inwards.

The brachialis anticus located in the front of the humerus or arm bone and the elbow flexes the forearm to commence the pull. The anterior fibres of the deltoid assist the arm forward, then the posterior fibres apply power to pull. Throughout the pull the wrist is kept firm by the flexor carpi radialis, situated on the inner side of the elbow, which flexes the wrist. When the arm approaches thigh level during the pull, power is applied by the teres major and minor situated on the shoulder blade. The latisimus dorsi, located along the lumbar and lower dorsal region of the back, between them draw the arm back under power and turn the humerus in its socket. When the pull is complete at about thigh level, the arm is raised from the water by the medial fibres of the deltoid together with the suprinatus muscles located in the shoulder blade and the trapiezius. The former rotates the arm away from the side while the latter lifts the shoulder blade upwards. The arm is then carried forward to re-enter the water, moved by the anterior fibres of the deltoid, again assisted by the pectoralis major and minor.

Whether the biceps in the front of the upper arm, or the triceps in the back of the upper arm are used during the pull will depend on whether the arm is bent or straight when pulling. If it is bent the biceps will give power and if it is straight then this will be supplied by the triceps. They will also be used with the anconeus at the back of the elbow to straighten the elbow so that the arm is straight when it enters the water to begin the pull.

Front crawl leg action
If the kick is to be effective the body must be well-balanced, and these muscles involved are the rectus abdominus, oblique externus abdominus, quadratus lumborum, oblique internus abdominus and the transversalis abdominus, all of which have already been mentioned. The erector spinae, which are located along the length of the spine and keep the spine erect while giving sideways flexion to the trunk, are also important. All these muscles assist in stabilising the pelvis during the kick. When done correctly the kick should commence in the hip joint, and it then uses the psoas muscle, located in the pelvic-lumbar region, which flexes the trunk on the thigh or the thigh on the trunk. The function which the muscle performs will depend on whether the feet are held or not; if the person is standing the trunk is flexed on the thigh, and if the feet are free the thighs are flexed on the trunk. The kick will start in the hip and run down the thigh, followed by a flexion of the knee joint by means of the popliteal muscle situated at the back of the knee, which causes relaxation in the quadriceps, made up of the vastus externus, vastus internus and crureus muscles located in the thigh. The lower leg is then kicked downwards, causing the biceps femoris on the back of the thigh and the hamstrings situated at the back of the knee joint to relax. On the down-kick, the foot is pointed backwards (plantar flexed)

by the peroneus brevis in the fibula or leg bone. This is also brought about by the flexors longus hallucis affecting the big toes, the flexors longus digitorum affecting the other toes, and the gastrocnemius or calf muscle which extends the foot and assists the knees to bend.

The soleus, located in the heads of the tibia and fibula, and the tibialis posticus, the deepest muscle in the leg also inverts or turns the foot inwards. In effect all the flexor and extensor muscles of the legs are used at some stage during the continual up-and-down movement of the legs.

Main muscles used in the breaststroke
From the breaststroke starting position with the hands in front of the chest the arms are pushed forward to their full stretch by means of the serratus magnus, located between the ribs and shoulder blades, the triceps at the back of the upper arm and the anconeus at the back of the elbow joint. The latter two muscles keep the elbows straight. During this movement the arms are kept to the midline of the body by the pectoralis major and minor, which are chest muscles mentioned earlier. During the sideways and downwards pull the pectorals and the posterior fibres of the deltoids apply power with the triceps keeping the elbows straight. When the pull is complete and the arms are sideways to the shoulder line they are drawn across the front of the chest by the biceps, the brachialis anticus and the coraco brachialis, both of which have already been mentioned. The latter assists the arm both forwards and inwards. From this position the arms are once again pushed forwards to recommence the stroke.

Breathing

Breath is usually taken in the breaststroke during the arm pull. The head is raised for breathing by the trapiezius and the splenius. Some swimmers tend to duck their heads forwards after breathing, and the power for this is supplied by the rectus capitus anticus major situated in the neck, which nods the head forward.

The leg action for the breaststroke is basically an unnatural movement, and thus the muscle action is a complicated one with almost every muscle in the leg being used at some stage. Most of the muscles involved have already been described so I will only give the location and function of those not already mentioned.

The thighs are flexed from a stretched position by the psoas muscle, while the lower legs are flexed by the hamstrings and gracialis located on the inner side of the thigh. The sartorius lies obliquely across the front of the thigh gastrocnemius. The plantaris is situated at the back of the knee joint and assists the gastrocnemius. The popliteus is also situated at the back of the knee joint. All these work together to flex the legs. As the knee bends, the feet are flexed with the toes towards the leg by the tibialis anticus, located on the outer side of the tibia. As the kick begins, the thighs are rotated outwards by the pyrformis, which is located partly within the pelvis and partly at the hip joint, and the obdurator internus in the same location. The obdurator externus covers the front wall of the pelvis and hip. The quadratus femoris is found at the front and inner side of the thigh.

As the thighs begin to rotate, they swing outwards to commence the kick. This abduction or movement outwards is powered by the gluteus minimus and gluteus medius. At the same time the quadriceps group at the front of the thigh, namely the rectus femoris vastus externus and internus and crureus extend the knee joint in the kick. At the end of the kick the foot is plantar flexed with the toes pushed downwards by the gastrocnemius soleus, plantaris and tibialis posticus with greater drive against the water being given by a final push through the toes by the flexor longus hallucis and flexor longus digitorum.

The muscles described for these two strokes are of course the main muscle groups supplying power. There are other smaller muscles which play their parts in these movements, but they cannot be described in this volume. The power in all strokes is supplied to a greater or lesser degree by those already mentioned. It must be remembered when teaching or learning swimming that the efficiency of muscle action basically stems from balance. The body always tries to balance itself, whether or not the movements it uses to do so are economical. This is instinctive, and thus the first skill to be mastered is that of balance. This will not be learnt until the mind is calm, because to balance properly one must be mentally relaxed.

Handicapped swimmers

Muscular action during swimming is highly complicated and inefficient muscular action rapidly leads to fatigue. I shall suggest some guidelines for working with handicapped pupils, although everything will of course depend on the pupil. His disability and the circumstances in which he is being taught are vital, and all work designed for him must fall within his physical range. This means that the teacher must know the pupil thoroughly, give him adequate rest, and always watch for signs of stress.

When you are dealing with a handicapped pupil, close attention must be paid to the type of movement you want him to do to achieve a particular desired objective. For example, in doing land therapy, an exercise designed and demonstrated on land would bear a direct relation to that exercise performed by the pupil on land. On the other hand an exercise demonstrated on land but performed in the water would have two different effects because of gravity. For example, if a pupil has a weakened deltoid and the exercise you set is raising the arm from the side to a sideways horizontal position to strengthen the muscle, the instructor demonstrating the movement on land would have to raise the arm against gravity and would thus derive a small amount of exercise from it. The pupil, although perhaps unable to perform this exercise on land, would have little difficulty in the water. If he was properly relaxed it would almost float to the surface, so the therapeutic strengthening value of the exercise would be small. Conversely the same exercise given to loosen a stiffened shoulder muscle would have greater theraputic value when done in water. The important point is that, when devising exercises for the handicapped, careful thought must be given to the exercise in relation to the medium in which it is to be performed.

Another common trap for the unwary is to assume that the place where someone feels pain or stiffness is the site of the lesion causing it. For example, if the pupil feels pain or stiffness in the fingers and he has recently hit his hand with a hammer, diagnosis should be relatively simple. On the other hand it could be that he is suffering from pressure on the ulna, medial or radial nerves leading from the brachial plexus near the neck. Never jump to conclusions, but always examine and question the pupil before reaching a final opinion, and then design the exercises.

Although I have stated in the chapter dealing with handicapped pupils that one must always consult the pupil's doctor about his suitability for waterwork, it does not necessarily follow that he is always the best person to advise you about the actual work to give him. In the field of muscular work there are specialists such as physiotherapists, masseurs and remedial gymnasts. If a knowledge of kinesology, the study of movement, is available, it could prove invaluable in helping to restore lost mobility to a joint or re-establish muscle tone. Your first and only consideration is the welfare and progress of your pupil, so always seek the best qualified advice.

Epilepsy

Thousands of children are now learning to swim in schools and clubs and through private tuition. There must be many among them who suffer from some debilitating disorder which produces no outward sign to the lay person, but which may be activated by physical stress or emotion. When a parent or guardian knows that a child suffers from such a condition it is their duty to inform the instructor concerned so that he can take special care of the child. This is especially important where school work is concerned, because a young and inexperienced teacher frequently has to take swimming lessons. If such a child collapses in the water it can be a frightening experience for all concerned. Any parent whose child has this problem should inform those who have temporary responsibility for him.

This has necessarily been a mere outline of anatomy and physiology as they relate to swimming. Those who are interested in this aspect of waterwork will find that there are several volumes on the subject available. Although the average reader may not want to go deeply into this complicated subject, I feel that anyone dealing with handicapped pupils should at least have an outline knowledge of what is happening to his pupil's body.

11

Teaching handicapped swimmers

This section dealing with swimming for the handicapped is included because sometimes teachers may have to deal with this type of pupil although they have no previous knowledge or experience. They should be aware of the dangers as well as the benefits of teaching a handicapped pupil to swim. This aspect of watermanship is least understood by the average person. Swimming for the handicapped is not the province of either the amateur or the swimming teacher. It is a matter for the doctor and the physiotherapist who are aided by the swimming teacher and this type of swimming is only really effective when all three bring their joint knowledge to bear on it. If they do not work together and cooperate fully it can be dangerous for the pupil.

Because of the medical safety aspect of handicapped swimming I emphasise that your first enquiries concerning your pupil's suitability for water work should be directed to his doctor. When the doctor agrees, and the physiotherapist has been fully informed, the swimming teacher can then apply his skills under their supervision. If you have to teach handicapped pupils without medical advice the following points should be remembered.

a   A handicapped pupil usually feels the cold very much, so the warmer the water is the better it is for him
b   If possible the same person should always be in the water with him, as this gives the pupil more confidence
c   Be lavish in praise however minute the progress your pupil makes
d   Have infinite patience and *never* try to rush him
e   Be firm as well as gentle
f   *Never* leave the pupil unattended. You must always be either in direct contact or within touching distance
g   The greater the pupil's incapacity the more detailed the attention he will need
h   Get to know the pupil thoroughly
i   *Never* work out of a safe depth: the maximum should be shoulder level

Many ailments, such as some respiratory conditions, certain types of paralysis, rheumatic and arthritic conditions, and simple asthmatic conditions respond well to hydrotherapy. On the other hand people with any mental disturbance, infective skin diseases or open wounds should not be given hydrotherapy. The safest policy is always to consult the pupil's doctor *before* swimming lessons commence rather than after, as irreparable damage may be done to the pupil's health.

Getting the pupil into the water

Entering the water can be a terrifying experience to a handicapped pupil. This is also a vital moment as one slip or accidental ducking at this stage may mean it will be very difficult for the pupil in the future. A successful first entry depends upon many factors such as the pupil himself, the nature of his disability and the availability of equipment. Because of these factors I will only stress the points which it may be helpful to remember when he enters the water for the first time.

a   Use a method suitable to the particular pupil's condition and incorporate aids if possible
b   *Do not* force your pupil. Be gentle but firm and don't confuse him
c   Be in *direct contact* with him throughout
d   Maintain this contact as he enters the water and while he is in it
e   If the operation is prolonged keep him as warm as possible
f   Do not lose your patience: remember that he is handicapped

The first entry

a   Keep in contact or within contacting distance of the pupil depending on his disability
b   Let him feel the water around him
c   If he can stand unassisted, teach him how to regain his feet from the prone and supine positions. His competence will depend on the nature of his disability and his confidence
d   Make the session short and check frequently to see if he is too cold
e   Chat quietly and confidently to him

Supporting the pupil in the water

Position yourself to the best advantage depending on the nature of the pupil's disability, with the aim of giving the pupil maximum support without interfering with his limb movements. Stand at the pupil's head and support him in one of these ways:

a   With one arm running down the centre of his back and the pupil's head resting on your shoulder, chest or upper arm. Use your free hand to stabilise his shoulder or arm

b   With both arms running under the pupil's shoulders and the hands supporting the middle section of his trunk. His head rests on your chest or shoulder

c   With your hands under his shoulders and his head resting on your upper forearms

d   With the pupil's head resting on the palm of one hand and your free hand supporting his upper trunk.

Your object at this stage is to make the pupil confident in your ability to support him and there are many manual ways of doing this, apart from the artificial aids which are now available. Everything will depend on his particular disability so you should experiment and try new methods of support. Work out whether they are functional and whether they will help this particular pupil. If so, use them: whether the method has been used before or not is completely irrelevant.

Gaining confidence in the water

Once the pupil is supported comfortably let him

a   Try stretching out, quietly insisting on normal breathing

b   Feel the water by being floated backwards

c   Try to get the legs moving in a gentle back crawl action with the arms sculling if his disability will allow this

d   Keep chatting quietly to him throughout

e   Float him with artificial aids but keeping direct contact. The pupil must know that he cannot sink so give him sufficient aids to make sure that he doesn't.

As he makes these leg and arm movements supported by aids the pupil will get a feeling of real achievement. These first hesitant steps are *extremely important*, so be alert to give *immediate* help at the slightest sign of difficulty.

Progress to more difficult exercises

Once he has gained a little confidence, help the pupil to progress to more difficult exercises within the limits of his disability. For example, if his legs are weak encourage him to

a   Bend and stretch while he is grasping the rail
b   Walk along sideways holding the rail
c   Walk forwards either holding your hand or grasping a stick you are holding
d   Walk one or two paces towards you or the rail but keeping within contacting distance
e   The use of very flexible flippers supported by aids will increase his leg strength in a back float when his confidence grows

Try to consult the physiotherapist and work out suitable exercises together.

After making some progress on the back, start on the exercises in the prone position. Because of breathing difficulties the use of prone strokes will depend on the pupil's specific disability. For example, weak neck muscles would indicate that work in this position was not advisable. If the pupil is able to work in the prone position make sure you give him immediate assistance if he loses his balance. Suitable aids can help the pupil to make gradual progress to doggy paddle or a crude trudgeon stroke. In these exercises it is advisable to place oneself either immediately in front of the pupil or alongside him so that you can always assist if necessary. When the pupil can manage this stage with reasonable success and confidence, start teaching him a suitable stroke. His stroke interpretation may bear little or no relation to the normal stroke but this is unimportant. Your objective is to teach him to move through the water by himself without using supports and if at all possible, to at least reduce his disability in the water.

Dealing with specific disabilities

Try to overcome the pupil's disability and assist him to get as near normality as possible. To achieve this the ends will justify the means and you should be guided by your pupil's needs and circumstances. Anything that will assist him is useful. Your greatest assets will be patience, ingenuity and the determination to overcome difficulties, but there are certain points which you must remember.

a Your pupil must always have unrestricted breathing
b Do *not* overwork your pupil
c Remove the pupil from the water at the *slightest sign* of distress
d *Always* take a doctor or physiotherapist's advice if you are in doubt
e Do *not* overstretch the pupil's muscle or group of muscles
f Vary your work to make it interesting
g Consult the doctor or physiotherapist before trying out new ideas
h Have a good fund of distracting small talk
i If the pupil is spastic or mentally handicapped, take things gently

Useful strokes for handicapped swimmers

The most suitable strokes for handicapped swimmers have already been described in detail, and this is a summary of suggestions:

a Life-saving backstroke with or without arm movements
b Surface-arm back stroke
c Adaptations of the breaststroke in the prone position
d Inverted breaststroke
e Adaptations of the front crawl such as doggy paddle and trudgeon
f Adaptations of the back crawl such as the hand scull and the underwater arm sweep and recovery

In a volume of this nature it is impossible to describe all the various disabilities or to give exercises relating to them, so I have grouped some of the more common disabilities and given suggestions for strokes or adaptations suitable for them. This is a highly individual process and the physiotherapist and swimming teacher should cooperate together to make a detailed analysis of the pupil's requirements along the lines I have suggested.

Weak neck muscles

These will be helped by any water-supported exercise as a continuation of the physiotherapist's land work. Try these exercises:

a   In a back float position using aids to support the pupil, practise raising and lowering the head
b   In a prone float position using aids, look at the rail on the opposite side
c   In a prone float position using aids, turn the head from side to side
d   In a back float position using aids put the float under the head and press it downwards

Later, when the pupil's neck strength has improved, a somer-saulting exercise could be introduced as follows:

a   Stand in shallow water up to chest level. Practise a front-somersault movement from the waist only to a tuck position and then stand up
b   Repeat exercise a doing a tuck handstand on the bottom
c   Repeat a springing from the bottom into a handstand
d   Push from the side and do a surface dive to an armstand
e   Push from the side and somersault to the feet
f   Repeat a springing and doing a full somersault to the feet.

In all of these exercises the head must be kept square and balanced.

Arm and shoulder disabilities

Start with exercises done in the supine position with the legs giving the main propulsion, such as the back crawl kick, the life-saving backstroke kick and the inverted breaststroke kick. The arms should at first perform a gentle sculling or sweeping movement, progressing to a fuller arm action as the pupil's strength grows. It is not advisable for any pupil to attempt a prone stroke until he has sufficient strength in his arms, and this will depend on the exact nature and degree of his disability. Many arm and shoulder exercises can be devised for shallow water with the pupil kneeling to bring the water up to his neck level. For example he can practise raising his arms sideways and forwards.

Disabilities of the upper trunk

A pupil disabled in the upper trunk may be injured or weak in the lattissimus dorsi, serratus posterior, infra-spinatus or the teres major or minor. All these muscles are important in the swimming arm action. The arms themselves would appear normal, but his pulling action would be impaired. His leg action would thus be the main source of propulsion, but if suitable exercises were devised to strengthen these muscles they could be brought into full play. Other water-supported exercises besides swimming movements may help in this restoration. For example try a mushroom float in a tight tuck position or a back float with the toes under the bar, rolling to a tight tuck and opening into a back float with or without support.

Weakness of the abdomen and lower trunk

Weakness of any of the abdominal muscles such as the psoas, rectus or transverse abdominus, or the external or internal obliques affects the swimming, especially the muscles used in respiration. When the pupil has these disabilities this indicates that strokes performed on the back would be easiest, but he should use water-supported exercises specially devised to assist him in recouping his abdominal strength. Any of the back-strokes, suitably adapted to his needs and taught with the support of aids, should eventually achieve results.

Disabilities of the legs

If your pupil suffers from a disability of the legs it is better to devote more of the early lesson on water-supported exercises to strengthening his limbs, before actually progressing to a swimming stroke. Get him to:

a   Bend and stretch holding the bar
b   Move sideways down the pool while holding the rail
c   Walk given distances
d   Hold the rail while jumping up and down.

The exercises you should use will depend on the location and degree of his disability. If his legs are too weak for such exercises, teach him to get into a back float position with aids and to use any of the modified backstroke leg kicks. Later he can progress to the use of flippers. If he has lost a limb he has the added problem of balance which must be taken into account before modifying any stroke.

Skeletal disabilities

Skeletal disabilities such as lordosis (hollow-back), kyphosis (hump-back), scoliosis (curvature of the spine), deformity after injury, and arthritic deformity are dealt with by the physio-therapist, who tries to strengthen the surrounding muscles to benefit the skeletal posture. All water work with pupils with this kind of disability should be a progressive continuation of the physiotherapist's work, using water-supported exercises and a swimming stroke which is applied directly to the deformity. For example, a pupil with kyphosis, which usually means a shortened pectoral muscle and limited shoulder movement, should use the back crawl, English backstroke, surface-arm backstroke and stretched back floating, together with adaptations of these movements.

Disabilities of the ankles and feet

A pupil suffering from a disability such as pes planus (flat feet), talips (club foot), or ankylosis of the ankle joint, which allows little mobility, should practise any exercise which will flex and extend the muscles. Any of the leg actions will help and the use of flippers, together with plenty of land work, will bring about greater mobility.

Teaching blind pupils

Blind pupils are not handicapped in the normal physical sense and should not be treated as if they were. They have a distinct advantage over the normal pupil in that they have the unique ability to concentrate absolutely. Once their initial fears are over they usually make rapid progress. Introduce a blind person to the water as follows, taking great care at this stage:

a   Acquaint the pupil with his new surroundings in detail
b   Let him get the feel of the places he will use
c   Let him explore the areas surrounding the bath, and answer any queries he may have
d   Allow him to get a mental picture of the distance involved with your guidance
e   Do not talk as though the pupil was half-witted

There are several ways of getting the blind pupil into the water, including these:

a   Sit on the side, reach down to grasp the rail and slide in backwards with his feet in contact with the wall until he reaches the bottom
b   As in a, except with the teacher standing behind him and resting his hand on the pupil's back to guide him

c Tell the pupil how many steps there are. Then he can hold the handrail with his back to the water. The teacher puts his hand on his back to guide him, while he feels his way down the steps or counts them out aloud

Accustoming a blind person to the water

Quiet and almost continuous talking as the teacher explains and encourages the pupil helps build his confidence at this stage. These exercises will help the pupil to familiarize himself with the pool:

a Walk along holding the rail and making occasional contact with the teacher for reassurance
b Hold the rail and practise submerging
c The teacher can guide him manually across the width of the pool counting the steps as they go
d Walk a few paces and return using vocal guidance only
e Keep within touching distance of the teacher but allow him to explore by himself while you keep talking
f If he is confident enough he can try submerging freely in shallow water. Maintain manual contact or keep within touching distance of the teacher

Choosing a stroke for blind swimmers

Once the pupil is at home in the water, teach him the floats, sculling, regaining the feet and how to get into the prone and supine positions to make him more confident before proceeding to actual stroke work. Because of the breathing problems during early stages, I have found it better to commence by teaching the back-stroke with the support of aids if required. Build up the leg action first with a hand-scull, until the pupil's confidence and balance is good. Then concentrate on arm action. When the pupil is proficient on his back, progress to the prone strokes. First do these at the rail with guidance and then with aids if necessary. Keep in close contact the whole time and talk reassuringly to the pupil.

Your pupil's progress will depend on the clarity of your verbal instructions. No detail is too fine to be ignored. Remember that the pupil must translate your words into a mental picture before he can transform his image into action. If your instructions are vague his ideas will be confused. If he is given sufficiently clear pictures of what he is being asked to do, he can progress normally through the strokes. Once they have the feeling of swimming many blind people produce almost startling results. The most difficult stage is the first time the pupil enters the pool, so you must take great pains to see that he is not frightened.

Introducing a deaf and dumb person to the water

Like the blind pupils deaf and dumb people are not handicapped in the physical sense and similarly they have tremendous powers of concentration. The greatest difficulty in this case is communication. Provided the teacher is adept at using his hands, eyes and body to mime and can either demonstrate the movement himself or get an assistant to do so, there should be little difficulty.

Useful aids for teaching the deaf and dumb are a blackboard, pencil and paper, pictures, a jointed model and lip-reading. To communicate by lip-reading it is essential that you face the pupil and speak *slowly*. Remember not to speak to the pupil as if he were half-witted. Once the pupil is confident and at home in the water, there is no physical reason why he should not progress through the normal stages of learning to swim, provided that you take care to give adequate and detailed demonstrations.

Handicapped swimming is a vast and complicated field with many possibilities and I regret that it is impossible to go into greater detail in this book. If, however, I have provided a guide to procedures then I will have at least achieved something. Hydrotherapy provides opportunities of improved health and pleasure for the handicapped but it has many pitfalls for the unwary. You *must* seek professional advice before undertaking such work. Consult the pupil's doctor and physiotherapist, and then you can coordinate their knowledge with your own teaching skills.

12

Diving: basic dives to the plain header

It is not the intention of this book to teach or explain advanced diving, but to describe the progressions towards it. Those who wish to learn advanced dives can consult one of the many volumes on the subject, notably George Rachkam's 'Diving'. I would also advise that you watch diving as often as possible and seek advice from a qualified teacher or coach.

Although the practices described here are progressive in themselves, it is not necessary to stick rigidly to them. Assess your pupil's ability and select the practices which are most suitable for him. Always arrange demonstrations whenever you can of the parts of a movement and the complete movement. For such demonstrations you will need a competent diver and visual aids such as pictures, jointed models, blackboards, pencil and paper, and film, if they are available. These are essential points to remember when you are teaching diving to beginners:

a   Ensure adequate safety
b   Maintain adequate discipline
c   *Always* work at a suitable depth for safety in relation to the pupil's ability
d   *Do not* allow or encourage the pupil to attempt dives beyond his ability
e   Make sure that any work which is attempted has been thoroughly prepared
f   Do not keep the pupil standing about when he is wet or cold
g   Do not bore or tire the pupil with constant repetition
h   Plan your programme and progressions so they are within the pupil's ability
i   Know your subject and be prepared to explain a movement to the pupil.

The pupil should start diving as soon as he has the ability to swim a standard length and in addition at least five yards underwater. He must also be able to understand and interpret detailed instructions, and be obedient. He should not start on a board or the side of the bath but in shallow water so he can gain experience in rotation and springing and build up his confidence.

Shallow water confidence exercises

Assuming that your pupil is an absolute beginner, these exercises will help to give him confidence and make him familiar with the underwater world:

a   Standing in shallow water up to chest level, put the face in with the eyes open
b   Repeat exercise a then touch the toes or pick up an object
c   Jump into the water with or without support. Crouch and then stand up
d   Push off from the side. Put the face in, glide through the water and then stand up
e   Push off from the side. Glide to the bottom, surface by turning the palms upwards and then raise the head
f   Start and finish as in exercise e, but glide between the partner's legs
g   Use the steps starting by sitting on the step at the water-line. Put the head down and the arms beyond the head. Tilt forward and push with the legs as the body tilts forward. Do a stretched glide underwater and then surface as in e. Repeat this working from a higher step each time
h   Stand in the water at chest level with the hands on the hips and sink to sit on the bottom. If this is difficult try jumping up before sinking and blowing air out slowly while sitting
i   Practise some mushroom floats
j   Do a pike float. Bend at the waist, keeping the arms and legs straight and holding the ankles
k   Practise various floats such as a mushroom to a straight float, then on to a pike float

Use any float or water game which involves having the pupil submerge, to vary the interest.

Rotation and springing

The ability to spring and rotate the body is essential to diving. Everyone can rotate, but the movement is set in motion by force

42 Touching the toes

43 Jumping in and crouching

44 Gliding to the bottom

45   Gliding between the partner's legs

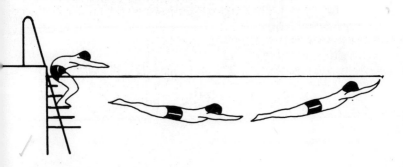

46   Starting from steps

outside the body. For example if you trip when walking downstairs, the body pitches forward head-first, and rotates. This rotation continues until another outside force stops it, for instance when you hit the ground. The speed of rotation depends on:

a   The take-off, which is the forward speed when the person tripped
b   The angle of take-off
c   The pressure applied upwards on the take-off, which determines the height reached
d   The position of the body on the take-off and whether it is straight or bent. Once rotation has been induced it can be slowed down by the body but not stopped.

132

47 Hands on the hips sink

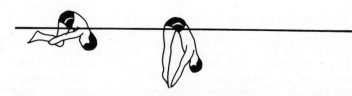

48 Mushroom and pike float

49 Variable floats

50–60   Rotation and springing exercises in shallow water

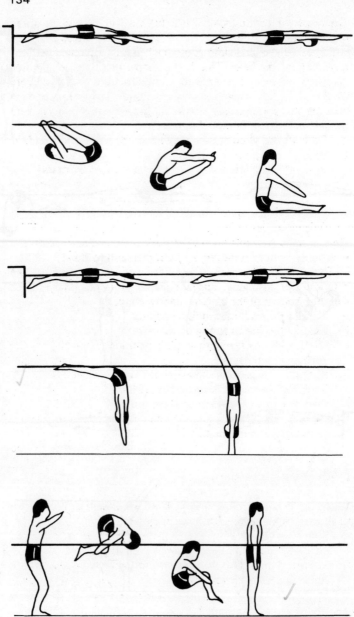

The body will rotate faster if it is bunched up or tucked, about half as fast when bent at the waist with the arms and legs straight or piked, and slowest of all when fully stretched with the arms beyond the head. This is the simple principle upon which diving is based and it embraces both forward and backward rotation. The following exercises are designed to give practice in creating this rotation and should all be done after a push from the side of the bath in shallow water:

a   Push off and glide putting the face in the water and stand up
b   Push off and glide then do a tuck somersault to stand
c   Push off and glide, doing a surface dive to an armstand
d   Push off and glide into a piked somersault ending sitting on the bottom
e   Push off and glide, then do a piked surface dive to an armstand

Devise other exercises on similar lines such as a surface dive, a tuck somersault to stand, or a pike somersault to stand.

The following exercises are designed to encourate both rotation and springing, and should be practised after a push from the bottom of the bath in shallow water:

a   Tuck somersault to standing position
b   Pike somersault to sitting on the bottom
c   Half-tuck somersault to a tuck position balancing on the bottom with the hands
d   Repeat exercise c and then stretch in to an armstand
e   Tuck dive to an armstand on the bottom
f   Pike dive to an armstand on the bottom

Devise other exercises which will enable your pupils to practise both springing and rotation.

Deeper water exercises

When the pupil is proficient in shallow water at chest level move to shoulder level for the following exercises:

a   Stand on the side of the bath and jump in in a tucked position. Spring off the bottom as high as possible
b   Starting with a push from the side or a prone float do a tuck somersault and then stand
c   Starting as in exercise b do a piked somersault to a standing position

61–71 Rotation and springing exercises in deeper water

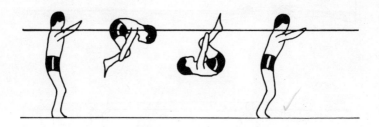

d   Start as in b and do a piked surface dive to an armstand

e   Push from the bottom, perform a pike surface dive to a crouching position and then spring to stand

f   Push from the bottom and do a piked somersault to a standing position

g   Push off from the bottom. Do one tuck somersault followed immediately by another one

h   Push off from the side of the bath and do two consecutive tuck somersaults to end standing up

i   Push off from the side on the back and do a back tucked somersault to a standing position

j   Push from the bottom doing a back tucked somersault to a standing position

k   Push off from the side moving through a piked back somersault into a standing position.

Work out other similar practices to do at this depth, to improve both spring and rotation.

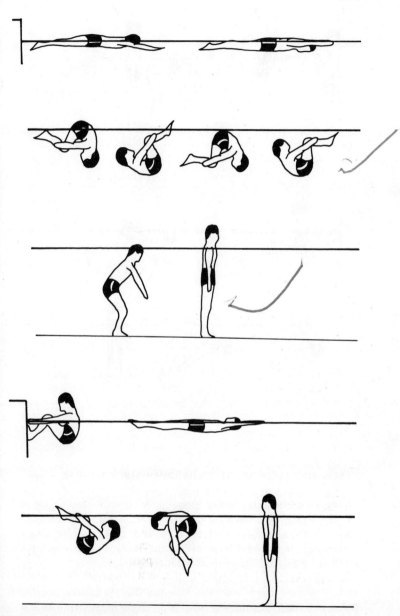

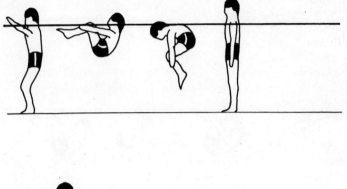

Water games for use with shallow water exercises

Flying porpoise: this water game is done individually. Do a piked surface dive to a crouching position then immediately spring into a second surface dive and crouch. Use single movements at first and then several consecutive ones. When the pupil has mastered the game make it competitive.

The dolphin: do a piked surface dive to just beneath the surface and then beat hard with the legs together just breaking the surface. Repeat this immediately. Use single movements at first and then several consecutive ones, once again making it competitive as the movement is mastered.

Ring dive: best done with the pupils in pairs. Stand sideways and make a circle with the arms. The pupil dives through this into a piked position.

Stick dive: standing in shallow water at chest level, hold the stick about two feet above the surface. Spring from the bottom and do a pike dive over it into a crouching position.

Sitting tag: can be done with one pupil or a pair. One chases the others and if their heads are above the surface when they are touched then they are out.

Tunnel dive: one, two or three pupils get in line, about half a yard apart, with their legs astride. Another pushes off from the side and glides through their legs.

Ring ball: arrange two teams in shallow water with the goalkeepers standing on either side of the width of the pool. They should be at the opposite end to their team. The rubber ring should be held shoulder high at arm's length and a swimmer has to get the ball through his own team's ring to score. You *must not* allow any ducking or pushing. If the swimmer is touched the ball must be passed.

Retriever race: collect an object from the bottom and return it to a specific place. Both teams should dive in together and they either have to retrieve a given number of objects in a set time or recover as many objects as possible.

Surface dive and the glide race: get into teams in shallow water. The pupils should stand one yard apart across the width of the pool with the alternate swimmers bending and placing their legs astride. The first pupil springs off the bottom, dives over the second to crouch on the bottom and then glides through the third one's legs. The whole team moves forward one yard and the movement is repeated until the team has finished.

Surface dives over the partner: the teams stand in shallow water and repeat the last exercise using bent positions only. Dive over to crouch and then immediately spring up and dive over the next in line. The team moves forward one yard and repeats this until everyone has had their turn.

Underwater obstacles course: the pupils work round an obstacle course, individually going through hoops or legs, under ropes and picking up objects.

Spot diving: two pupils holding a rubber ring stand three or four yards apart. The nearest one should be about two yards from the side and the minimum depth should be shoulder level. Dive through the first ring and surface through the second one. Ensure that the water is deep enough for shallow diving and also that the rings are fairly large.

These are only some of the many games which can be played incorporating under water work, springing and rotation to build up the pupil's confidence. When you are working with a class you must maintain strict discipline and make safety your first consideration at all times. When the pupil can confidently spring and rotate, the following progressions can be used to lead to the key or basic dives. If you are teaching beginners make sure that one pupil has surfaced before the next one dives and always keep in full control of the class.

The sitting dive

To do the sitting dive, sit on the side of the bath resting the feet either on the rail or in the scum channel. The trunk should be rounded forward with the head on the chest. The arms are stretched beyond the head in line with the ears and the wrists or forearms just touch the knees. Sometimes this dive is taught with the trunk straight and the arms above the head, but this is not always effective with beginners because it can cause mis-timing of the movement and result in a short entry or a belly flop.

The body tilts forward to overbalance and at the moment of overbalance the legs push vigorously. The body enters the water stretched and straight and holds this position under water. Re-surface by raising the head and turning the palms upwards.

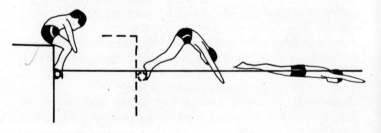

72   Sitting dive

Practices

a   Demonstrate each section of the dive and then the complete movement
b   Place the pupil in the correct position on the side of the bath
c   On the instruction 'tilt', the body overbalances and at the moment of overbalance call out 'push' to remind the pupil to do a fast leg extension
d   Get one pupil at a time to practise the complete skill

Points to watch for with beginners

a   Good tuck position on the side
b   Feet on the rail or channel
c   Keep the head down
d   Fast leg push
e   Stretched position in flight and under water
f   Re-surfacing technique should keep the head up and the palms raised
g   You must instruct the pupil to push at the right moment

The kneeling dive
The kneeling dive is not always a necessary progression but is included here to give continuity. The pupil places one foot on the edge of the bath with his toes curled over. He kneels on the other knee in line with the instep of the first foot. His trunk is rounded forward and his head in line with the curve of the trunk. The chin rests on the chest and the arms are beyond the head in line with the ears.

The body tilts but when overbalancing is about to occur the foot on the side of the bath pushes hard. The kneeling leg should assist in the push as it straightens and joins the other one in flight. The body is stretched during flight and entry. The under water and re-surfacing parts of this dive are the same as for the sitting dive.

Practices

a   Demonstrate each section of the dive and the complete movement

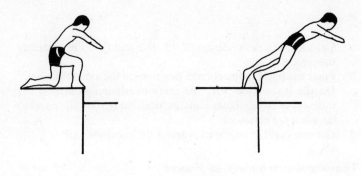

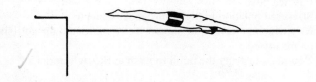

73   Kneeling dive

b   Place the pupil in the correct position on the side of the
    bath. Check the position of his forward foot and the knee of
    his rear leg
c   When told to 'tilt', the body overbalances. At the moment of
    over-balance call out 'push' to remind him to make a fast leg
    extension
d   Get one pupil at a time to practise the complete skill

Points to watch for with beginners

a   Foot on the edge with the toes curled over
b   Knee of the kneeling leg in line with the instep of the
    forward leg
c   Do not sit back onto the rear leg
d   Keep the chin to the chest during the dive
e   Keep the arms straight

f   Make sure the curve of the trunk is comfortable
g   Give the instruction 'push' at the correct point of over-balance
h   Vigorous leg push
i   Stretched flight and entry
j   Shallow entry
k   Legs together and stretched for entry
l   No head-lift for entry

The lunge dive

The lunge dive is not always the next dive to be taught but it has been included at this point in the chapter to give greater continuity. The pupil stands with one foot on the edge with his toes curled over it and his knees slightly bent. The other leg should be comfortably behind him so he is balanced on the ball of his foot with the knee slightly bent. The trunk is rounded forward and the head follows the line of the trunk with the chin on the chest. The arms are stretched beyond the head in line

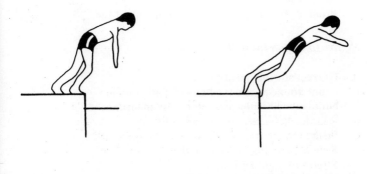

74   Lunge dive

with the ears and pointing towards the water. The eyes look forwards and downwards.

The pupil tilts forwards to overbalance and at the moment of overbalance the forward leg pushes hard. The rear leg assists in the push as it straightens and joins the other one in flight. The body is stretched throughout the flight, the entry and the underwater glide. Re-surface with the palms and the head up. The entry for this dive should be slightly further away from the side of the bath.

Practices

a   Demonstrate each section of the dive and the complete dive
b   Place the pupil in the correct position on the side of the bath. Check the position of his rear leg and the knee-bend in both legs
c   On the instruction 'tilt' the body overbalances. At the moment of overbalance give the push signal for a fast leg extension
d   Practise the complete skill, one pupil at a time

Points to watch for with beginners

a   Correct starting position
b   Trunk rounded and the head and arms in line
c   No overbend in the legs, especially the front leg
d   Rear leg balanced on the ball of the foot
e   Push at the correct point when overbalancing
f   Rear leg coming into line in flight
g   Stretched flight and entry
h   No head-lift for entry
i   Angle of entry
j   Entry point should be five or six feet from the side

The crouch dive
The crouch dive can usually be attempted as soon as the pupil can do a satisfactory sitting dive. The pupil takes up a low crouching position on the side of the bath with his toes curled over the edge. The trunk should be comfortably rounded forwards with the head following the trunk line and the chin to

the chest. The arms are stretched beyond the head in line with the ears and pointing towards the water.

The pupil tilts forwards to overbalance but at the moment of overbalance the legs push vigorously against the side of the bath. The body is stretched for the flight, the entry and the

75　Crouch dive

underwater part of the dive. Re-surface with the palms and head up.

The entry for this dive should be three to four feet from the side of the bath at this stage. For the later stages of the crouch dive the entry point is brought progressively closer to the side.

Practices

a   Demonstrate each phase and the complete dive
b   Place the pupil in the correct position on the side of the bath. Check the position of his bottom, which should be in line with the heels
c   The body overbalances when he is told to tilt. At the moment of overbalance the teacher should tell the pupil to push for a fast leg extension
d   Practise the complete skill one at a time

When the crouch dive has been mastered repeat the practices, gradually straightening the pupil's legs in the take-off position, until he is in a standing position with only a *partially* rounded trunk.

Points to watch for with beginners

a   Correct starting position
b   Do *not* stick the bottom backwards beyond the heels
c   No leaning forwards until the tilt phase
d   Feet not too far apart, in line with the hips
e   Check arm position
f   Head down and no head lift in flight or entry
g   No kicking up of the lower legs on take-off. Drive through the hips
h   Push at the correct point in the overbalance
i   Vigorous leg push
j   Toes pointed in the take-off
k   Stretched flight and underwater phase

The plunge dive
Once the crouch dive has been straightened to achieve a full standing take-off, the plunge dive should prove quite easy to accomplish. The pupil stands straight-legged on the side of the bath with his toes curled over the edge. The trunk should be comfortably rounded with the head following the line of the trunk. The arms hang loosely from the shoulders.

All the movements involved in the plunge dive should take place continuously. At the same time as the body tilts forward, the knees bend and the arms swing backwards. As soon as the body reaches the point of overbalancing the legs push vigor-

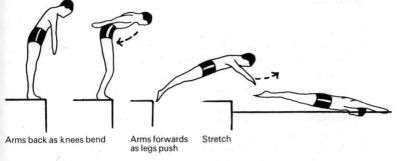

Arms back as knees bend   Arms forwards   Stretch
as legs push

76 Plunge dive

ously and the arms swing forward in line with the trunk. The head is between them. The body is kept fully stretched as contact is lost and remains stretched throughout the flight and entry. The entry for this dive should be five or six feet away from the side of the bath and the underwater glide should be held as long as possible.

Practices

a   Demonstrate each section of the dive and the whole movement
b   Practise the simultaneous tilt, the bending of the knees and the arm backswing on land. Stand in front of the pupil and place your hands on his chest for support
c   On the side of the bath repeat exercise b slowly, with the teacher hold a towel around the pupil's chest from the rear to support his body
d   Practise the stretched take-off on land especially the leg extension and the forward swing of the arms. Hold a towel around the pupil's chest from the rear to give support. Do this slowly to allow time to coordinate the arms and legs
e   Repeat d and c on the side of the bath. Practise a full take-off at half-speed and then the teacher should check the coordination of the pupil's movements
f   Repeat exercise at full speed. Shout 'push' at the moment when the arms swing through the hip line. The pupil should reach the farthest stretch with his full leg extension

Points to watch for with beginners

a   Correct starting position
b   Do not bend the knees too much in the take-off
c   Shoulders kept over the hips in the 'tilt' phase
d   Correct coordination of the tilt, knee-bend and backswing
e   Correct coordination of the forward arm-swing and leg-stretch in the push-off
f   Stretched flight, as contact is lost and during entry
g   Drive through the hips and do not kick upwards
h   Arms in line with the ears on take-off
i   No head-lift in flight or entry
j   Stretched position under water

The plain header

To achieve a good plain header takes considerable practice. Usually the pupil is taken through the spring header before attempting the true plain header. There are two differences between these dives. The starting position for the plain header is with the body upright but for the spring header the body is bent slightly at the waist. The entry for a plain header should be as near to the side and as vertical as possible. For the spring header this should be between three and four feet from the side and as near vertical as possible. All other phases of this dive are the same as for the plain header. The spring header stage assists the pupil to perform a correct take-off by driving up through his hips to rotate.

The pupil stands erect on the side of the bath with the toes curled over to grip it. The arms are raised at an angle of 45 to 50 degrees beyond the head, which should be balanced and unstrained with the eyes looking straight ahead. The palms face the water.

The movements should take place as one continuous motion without a pause in any phase. The body tilts forward to the balls of the feet with the knees bending slightly. As the body tilts just beyond the vertical, the legs push vigorously. At the same time the trunk bends slightly at the waist, although the head and arm positions remain unchanged. This bend is maintained as the feet leave the side of the bath. The body rotates through half a somersault in this position until just prior to entry. When he is about to enter the water the pupil's legs come into line with the

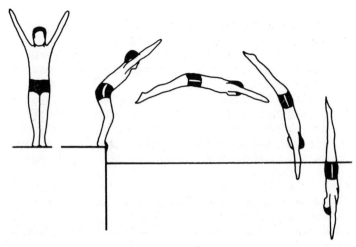

Start Tilt   Hold slight bend. Legs into bend

77   Plain header

trunk, the arms close and the body is stretched in a straight line.
The entry should be as vertical as possible.

Practices

All practices should be performed in a safe depth because of
vertical entries. The minimum depth should be ten feet if
possible and if it is below this alter the angle of entry to suit the
depth. For every ten degrees of entry angle the pupil will gain
roughly one foot of water depth. If the depth available is six feet:

Vertical entry at 90 degrees equals 6 feet   unsafe
          entry at 80 degrees equals 7 feet   unsafe
          entry at 70 degrees equals 8 feet   minimal safety
          entry at 60 degrees equals 9 feet   safer
          entry at 50 degrees equals 10 feet   safe

If the pupil were to strike the bottom in a vertical position he
could break his wrists. If he uses an angled entry he will plane
along the bottom if he strikes it.

Practices

a   Demonstrate the whole dive and each section of it
b   In shallow water, return to the springing and rotation exercises for revision, ensuring good leg thrust
c   Practise the starting position on land and the vertical leg thrust standing on land while holding the pupil from both sides with a towel around his waist. A pupil should be in front for chest support
d   Practise the take-off movement, thrusting through the hips
e   At the side of the bath, slowly practise the take-off movement and check the timing of the tilt and leg-push. The towel should be around the pupil's chest and held from the rear to provide support
f   Full take-off movement into the water. The teacher should check the timing making sure the pupil drives through the hips with the legs straight on take-off
g   Full dive with the teacher checking the take-off, flight and entry
h   To gain height hold a towel or stick in front of the pupil on the take-off. Place it about two feet high and six inches from the side of the bath. Increase the height but not the distance as the pupil's ability grows

Points to watch for with beginners

a   Safe depth
b   Take-off angle should be upwards not outwards
c   No leaning forward on the take-off
d   No kicking-up with the heels on the take-off
e   Push at the correct phase of the tilt movement
f   Final drive through the toes with the legs straight together
g   Keep the head and arms in line on the take-off
h   Drive up through the hips
i   Good coordination of movements
j   Slight bend at the waist until just prior to entry
k   Body brought into line when entry is imminent
l   Entry as near vertical as possible

Most faults which occur in the plain header are the result of a poor take-off. Check that this is correct in the early stages so that your pupil will develop a good dive.

Conscientious work during the early teaching of diving will produce the mastery of techniques required to do the key dives in the next section. Sloppy or inefficient work at this stage will immediately be apparent in the more advanced dives. No diving pupil should be allowed to attempt spring-board work until this stage has been thoroughly mastered and he has been taught running and standing take-offs from the spring-board.

13

Identification and marking of dives

As an introduction to advanced diving, a brief explanation of the identification and marking of dives and a description of the key dives follows. Also included is an illustrated list of exercises to be performed on the side of the bath, which are essential for learning the key dives and more advanced work.

All dives belong to one of the two dive tables: the spring-board and the high-board. They are all divided into groups according to the direction of the take-off. The spring-board has five and the high-board six groups:

(1) forward take-off with forward rotation
(2) backward take-offs with back rotation
(3) reverse take-off facing the water with backward rotation
(4) inward take-off with the back to the water and forward rotation
(5) twist dives are any of the above take-offs with a twist in the dive

High-board groups are the same as for the spring-board, except for one extra group of armstand take-offs.

Dive numbers

All dive numbers are arrived at by a combination of the following:

a   The direction of take-off (which group it is from)
b   Whether the dive contains a flying movement
c   The number of half-somersaults in the dive
d   The number of half lateral turns or twists in the dive
e   Whether the position in which the dive is performed is (A) straight, (B) piked, (C) tucked, or (D) twisted

Examples of dive numbers

a   Forward dive in the straight position: number 101A
    1   forward group

0 no flying movements in the dive
1 one-half somersault, so the diver takes off from his feet and enters head-first
A performed straight
b Flying inward one and a half somersaults tucked: number 413C
    4 inward group
    1 one flying movement in the dive
    3 three half somersaults in the dive
    C performed in the tuck position
c One and a half forward somersaults with two twists: number 5134D
    5 twist group
    1 forward movement
    3 three half somersaults in the dive
    4 four half lateral turns in the dive
    D performed in a position to suit the diver

The diving tariff

In addition to its identification number, which remains the same for competition work throughout the world, each dive has a tariff which is arrived at by assessing the difficulty of the complete movement, the board which is used, and the position in which it is performed.

Tariffs
Forward dive number 101 is performed from

springboard	Tarriffs
A position on the 1-metre board	1.4
B or C position on the 1-metre board	1.2
A position on the 3-metre board	1.6
B or C position on the 3-metre board	1.3
Highboard	
A position on the 5- to $7\frac{1}{2}$-metre board	1.4
B or C position on the 5- to $7\frac{1}{2}$-metre board	1.3
A position on the 10-metre board	1.6
B or C position on the 10-metre board	1.4

158

It is considered more difficult to execute the dive correctly from both the 10-metre high-board and the 3-metre spring-board in the 'A' position.

Reverse somersault number 302

From 1-metre: Position A—2.0 Position B—1.8 Position C—1.6

From 3-metre: Position A—1.9 Position B—1.7 Position C—1.5

It is considered most difficult to perform the reverse somersault from the 1-metre spring-board in the straight position.

Final marks in competition

In competition, marks are awarded in half points from 0 to 10. If there are three judges marking their marks are totalled together and the result is multiplied by the tariff given to the dive in the tariff table. Three judges are usually employed in local competitions, but because of the possibility of favouritism when all the marks are counted this is not considered to be entirely satisfactory.

When there are five judges marking the highest and lowest marks awarded are disregarded in the total. The total of the three remaining judges is then multiplied by the tariff as before, for example:

Five judges' marks:

	1	2	3	4	5
Marks	$4\frac{1}{2}$	5	$5\frac{1}{2}$	2	6

The marks of judges four and five would be entered on the diver's record sheet, but are to be ignored. The total marks from the remaining judges would total 15. If the dive was a forward straight dive, such as dive 101A performed from the 1-metre board at a tariff of 1.4, the judges' total of 15 marks would be multiplied by 1.4 giving a final mark of 21.00.

Each dive is recorded as above on the competition dive sheet, with a running total kept after each dive. In this way the officials, spectators and divers can be fully aware of their position throughout the contest. Five judges are used in all championship contests and this is considered more satisfactory since it offsets any bias for or against any particular diver.

In many international contests seven judges are used and their marks are calculated as follows:

(6) 5 5 5 5 5 (5) = 25 × tariff 2·0 = 50 ÷ 5 = 10 × 3 = 30

So that the final mark awarded for the dive is 30. In all Amateur Swimming Association competitions divers must perform five set dives and a number of voluntary dives according to the rules set for that competition.

14

The key dives and diving exercises

The key dives are all performed in the B or piked position except the twist dive, which is performed in the A or straight position. They are the forward, backward, reverse and inward dives and the forward dive straight with one twist. The reason why these dives have been chosen as the key dives for learning advanced work is that they can all be performed from a near-vertical take-off position and the performer can clearly display his degree of control over the movements. This does not mean that the key dives have to be learnt first, but to prepare for advanced work it is better if they are.

The high-board has two further key dives in addition to the above:

a   The armstand somersault in the C or tucked position. From a handstand start position, with a head-first entry

b   The armstand cut-through in the C or tucked position. Start from a handstand position and, as the body overbalances forward, it is tucked with the legs being brought down between the arms. The body is then straightened with the arms to the sides and the diver enters the water feet-first

Since the objective of this book is to teach only the elementary stages of the skills which are dealt with, it would defeat its purpose to detail the teaching practices for key dives, as they are the beginnings of advanced diving. This also applies to the teaching of the hurdle step which is essential to advanced spring-board diving. Both these subjects require more technical teaching of balance, coordination and timing. I shall only give a description of the basic movements involved in the dives, but to assist those who wish to go further into these dives, I have included a series of illustrated bathside exercises. If they are mastered correctly the pupil will be able to perform the key dives from a standing take-off on the 1-metre spring-board.

The forward dive pike

Take-off is forwards, and as the body rises from the board, it bends at the waist. The arms are held straight and the hands touch the feet, so that the body is piked. The body is then unpiked by bringing the legs upwards in line with the trunk. At the same time as this leg movement the arms, still held straight, are taken beyond the head, so that the whole body is now in line for entry. No bend in the knees is allowed in any part of the movement and the legs are kept together throughout.

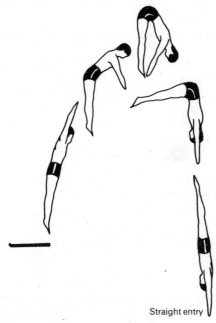

Straight entry

78   Forward dive pike

The back dive pike
The take-off is backwards, and as the body rises up and away from the board the legs are raised until the feet are above head level. The hands touch the feet with the arms held straight so the body is piked. As the body begins to fall it is unpiked. The legs remain still but the trunk is dropped towards the water. The arms are simultaneously taken beyond the head so that the whole body is now in line for entry. No bend is allowed in the knees in any phase of the dive and the legs should be kept together throughout.

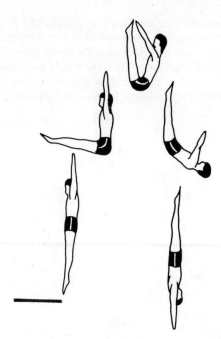

79   Back dive pike

The reverse dive pike
The take-off is forwards, with a slight backwards rotation. As
the body rises up and away from the board, the legs are raised
until they are above the level of the head. The arms are held
straight so the hands can touch the feet, bringing the body into a
piked position. As the body begins to fall it unpikes. The legs
remain still and the trunk is dropped towards the water. At the
same time the arms are taken beyond the head so the whole
body is now in line for entry. No bend is allowed in the knees in
any section of the movement and the legs are held together
throughout.

The inward dive pike
Take-off is backwards, with a slight forwards rotation. As the
body rises up and away from the board the trunk bends
downwards at the waist so the body is piked. The body is then

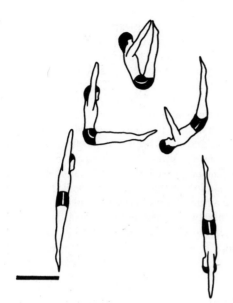

80 Reverse dive pike

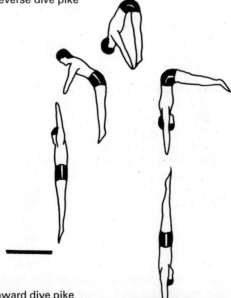

81 Inward dive pike

unpiked by bringing the legs upwards in line with the trunk. At the same time as this leg movement the arms, still kept straight, are taken beyond the head. The whole body is now in line for entry. Do not bend the knees and keep the legs together throughout the movement.

Forward dive straight with one twist
The take-off is forwards. The body rises straight to the highest point of the dive, and as it begins to fall it is twisted about its long axis and sideways through a full circle, by using the arms and shoulders. The arms are immediately taken beyond the head for entry. No bending of the body is allowed in any part of the movement. The actual point of twisting will vary from one diver to another. Some twist early in the forwards movement and others twist late, but whenever the twist is taken the body must remain straight.

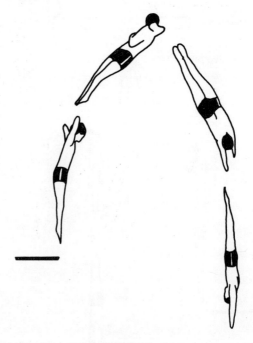

82   Forward dive with one twist

The armstand somersault on a firm board
Take-off for this dive is from a handstand with the back to the water. The handstand must be clearly held before the dive is made. As the body overbalances and loses contact with the board it is tucked, and then almost immediately untucked to bring it into a straight line ready for entry.

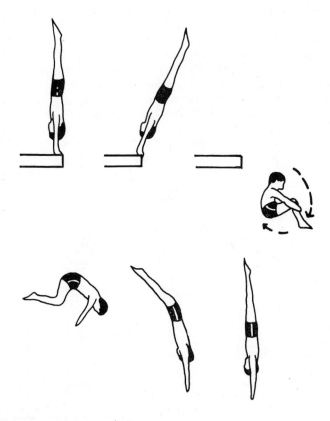

83   Armstand somersault

The armstand forward cut-through
The take-off is from a handstand with the back to the water. The handstand must be clearly held before the dive is made. As the

body begins to overbalance and lose contact it is tucked momentarily and then the legs are brought down between the arms until the body is straight with the arms to the sides. The entry is feet-first. The overbalance and tuck through to the straight position must be virtually simultaneous to be effective.

Exercises to be practised on the side of the bath

It is essential to have strict supervision when performing the following exercises. This is *especially* so with the reverse and inward movements. If the side of the bath is slippery, wet a towel, wring it out and hang it over the edge of the side for added safety. When you are teaching a class have your pupils *well spaced out* and give personal attention to each diver when he is diving. Stand either immediately in front of or behind the diver to ensure that he does not strike the side of the bath. It is also essential that strict discipline is maintained when working on diving exercises with beginners. No pupil should be allowed to perform an exercise until the previous pupil has surfaced.

Forward exercises

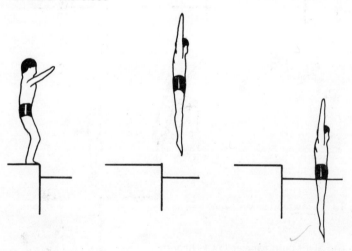

84   Straight jump

167

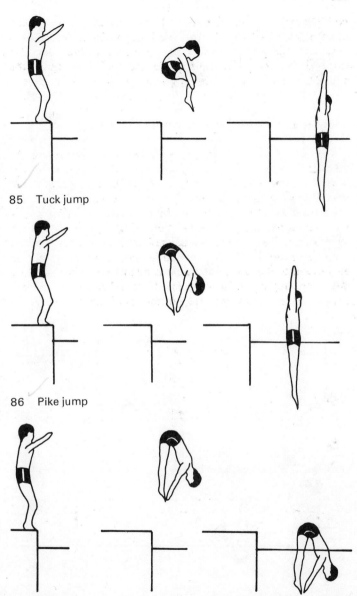

85   Tuck jump

86   Pike jump

87   Pike drop

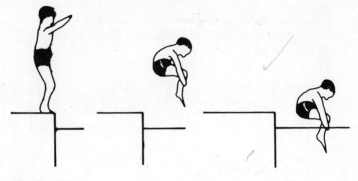

88 Tuck drop

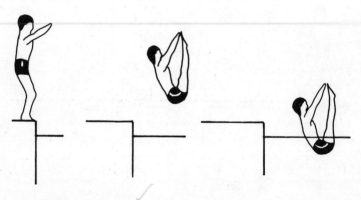

89 Piked seat drop

90 Forward roll

91 Crouch tuck roll with leg push

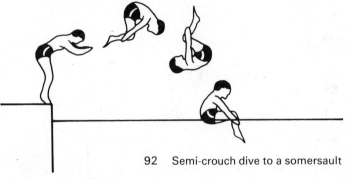

92 Semi-crouch dive to a somersault

93 Spring somersault

94 Running front somersault

95 Forward dive tuck

96   Forward dive pike

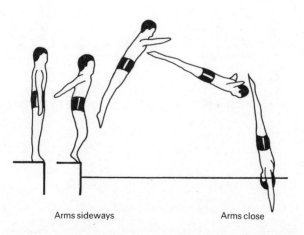

Arms sideways   Arms close

97   Forward dive straight with arm swing

If facing right push the left shoulder forward and the right one backward and vice versa. Use hip twist to assist. Keep the arms sideways until they close for entry

98   Standing half twist

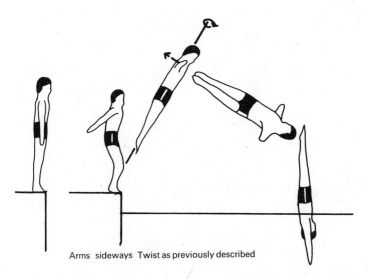

Arms sideways Twist as previously described

99 Forward dive half twist

Use the shoulders as described. Bring one arm across the chest and press the other elbow backward on the back of the head. Twist must be fast

100 Forward dive on twist

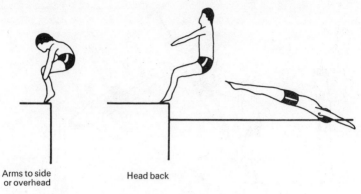

Arms to side
or overhead

Head back

101 Back roll tuck with stretched entry

Head back

102 Crouch back dive

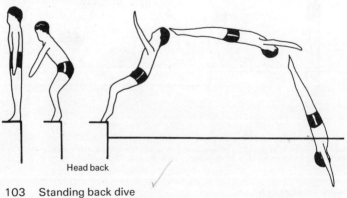

Head back

103 Standing back dive

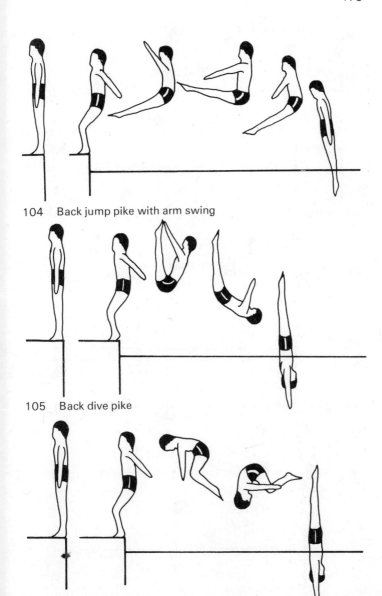

104 Back jump pike with arm swing

105 Back dive pike

106 Inward dive tuck

176

107   Inward dive pike

108   Reverse dive tuck

109   Reverse pike jump

110 Reverse pike drop

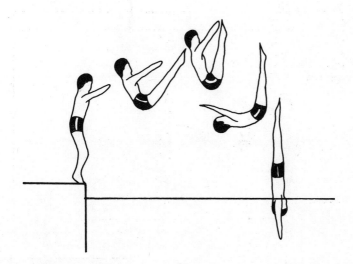

111 Reverse dive pike

Enter with one foot first

112 Reverse kick jump

Enter with both legs together

113 Reverse kick jump

114 Reverse kick dive

Summary on diving

The introduction to the key dives ends this section on teaching beginners. However as far as diving itself is concerned it is only the very beginning, for diving is not just a sport, it is an art requiring courage, determination, ability and above all constant practice. In no other sport except gymnastics has the performer so little time in which to complete a complicated aerial movement. He must be right first time as he has only about one and a half seconds in which to do the dive.

If you wish to know more about this fascinating art, watch it and learn to understand the finer points. Judge dives for yourself, ask questions from coaches or divers, but do not try to copy the movements of an experienced trained diver after watching for a few brief minutes. His movements are the results of months or even years of constant practice.